GREEN DIESELS IN VIEW

MICHAEL WELCH

Rails

Contents

Title page: Train movements at weekends are reduced compared to mid-week and many locomotives can be found stabled at depots or yards. This picture was taken at Crewe North stabling point on Sunday 23rd July 1967 and shows a trio of English Electric Type 4s with No.D249, nearest to the camera, No.D205 and part of No.D292 just creeping into the picture on the left. Two Brush Type 4s complete this typical scene from the green diesel era. No.D205 was one of a handful of these 2,000hp locomotives that entered service at Stratford shed in east London in early 1958 for use on the expresses from Liverpool Street to Norwich. Regrettably, it had the dubious distinction of having one of the shortest careers of any member of the class, being withdrawn in January 1976 some time before the withdrawal programme for the class began in earnest. It was broken-up at Crewe works, just a stone's throw from where this shot was taken, in February 1977. No.D249 made its debut in traffic at Gateshead in November 1959 and survived until early 1983. *Rail Photoprints*

Published by Rails Publishing
www.railspublishing.com

ISBN 978 1 85414 439 3

Printed by Parksons Graphics

© Michael Welch 2019

Front Cover: The neat and tidy appearance of Clarbeston Road is ample testament to the pride local staff clearly took in maintaining their station. A 'Hymek' diesel hydraulic B-B locomotive, No.D7083, is seen pausing with a one-coach Fishguard Harbour to Whitland train on 15th August 1963. The station here, named after a small hamlet two miles distant, is actually a junction where the branch to Fishguard diverges from the main line to Milford Haven. *Noel Machell*

Introduction

On 18th December 1947 Great Britain's first main line diesel locomotive, 1,160hp Co-Co No. 10000, was shown off to the press and public at Euston station and later made a short trip to Watford and back to demonstrate its capabilities. It had been constructed by the LMS working in association with English Electric under the direction of H.G. Ivatt; a sister locomotive, No.10001, emerged from Derby works in July 1948. In November 1950 a 1,750hp 1Co-Co1 locomotive, No.10201, entered traffic and this was followed by a further example whilst a third similar, but more powerful, machine took to the rails in March 1954. All of these locomotives entered service painted black but the unimaginative policy of painting diesels in drab, uninspiring black livery was not destined to last much longer.

In October 1956 the railway periodical *Trains Illustrated* reported 'It is gratifying to learn that the protests at the unprepossessing black livery so far applied to British diesels have had effect' and the magazine gleefully reported that visitors to Derby works on August 19th had spotted all five main line diesels in the works of which Nos.10000 and 10201 were 'in the paint shop newly liveried green'. The good news was not confined to the main line fleet and the fact that diesel shunter No.13260 was also to be turned out in 'the new style', in preference to plain black, was certainly reassuring and probably widely acclaimed. So it seemed that locomotives of all shapes and sizes were to be painted in Brunswick green in future thus joining the fleets of DMUs that had sported green livery from the outset. The secret was out and it was clear that the days of BR diesel locomotives sporting dull black livery were well and truly over.

During 1955 British Railways had announced the details of a modernisation plan which included the replacement of steam by diesel and electric traction at an approximate cost of £1,500m. over a fifteen year period. The BR management took the view that steam traction was not capable of further development and opted for more modern motive power which, it was anticipated, would offer better availability, economy and, most importantly, much faster point to point journey times which were essential to combat increasingly stiff competition in the transport industry. BR's lack of experience with modern traction prompted a considered, cautious approach and it was decided to order 174 'pilot scheme' diesel locomotives in various power categories to assess their capabilities. in June 1957 the first fruits of this policy started to have tangible results when the very first locomotive constructed under the modernisation scheme rolled off the production lines. The railway enthusiast fraternity must have doubted whether the new edict regarding liveries had filtered down to the manufacturers, English Electric Co., but in the event they need not have worried because when Type 1 1,000hp Bo-Bo No.D8000 was unveiled it was resplendent in a newly applied coat of green paint!

It's been a real pleasure compiling this album which would never have reached completion without the help of many photographers who provided a host of wonderfully evocative images. Bob Dalton, Chris Evans, Dave Fakes and Terry Phillips have scrutinised the proof and suggested many amendments and worthwhile improvements. The following gentlemen have kindly made available photographs from collections in their care, Richard Barber (Armstrong Railway Photographic Trust), John Chalcraft (Rail Photoprints), Rodney Lissenden (R.C. Riley collection), Allan Trotter (Eastbank Model Railway Club) and Peter Waller (Online Transport Archive).

Michael Welch
Burgess Hill, West Sussex
October 2019

Derby-built 'lightweight' units

British Railways' first tentative steps into conventional DMU operation were made in the West Riding of Yorkshire on 14th June 1954 when a fleet of eight 2-car 'Derby Lightweight' units took over the operation of local trains between Leeds and Bradford. These units were based at Bradford (Hammerton Street) depot which, arguably, was BR's first diesel depot though it also continued to maintain steam traction until 1958. Both vehicles were equipped with two 125hp Leyland engines so the units, which worked over a steeply graded route, were particularly powerful. A further series of 'Derby Lightweight' units with the usual combination of one motor and one trailer vehicle was built later in 1954, the motor coaches only being fitted with two BUT 150hp engines because it was considered that the units did not need as much power as the earlier batch. These units were constructed in one-, two- and four-car formations for the London Midland (LMR), Eastern (ER) and North Eastern Regions (NER), the last mentioned series being earmarked for the NER. The unit nearest to the camera in this portrait taken at York on 1st September 1962 is a four-car example, five of which entered traffic in September 1955 at South Gosforth depot near Newcastle-upon-Tyne. The leading carriage is a Driving Motor Composite (DMC) which consisted of a 12-seat first class saloon for smokers, immediately behind the driving cab, this being separated from an 8-seat, non smoking, first class saloon by a vestibule. The rest of the coach contained 36 seats for second class passengers, but no lavatory accommodation. Quite apart from this comparatively rare and most interesting DMU, this view vividly illustrates the incredible variety of traction that could be seen on the network at that time. A Metropolitan-Cammell DMU can be seen lurking in the station together with a Brush Type 2 locomotive and a small diesel shunter, but pride of place must surely go to the Gresley Class A4 Pacific, the front end of which is just visible. The tracks curving sharply away to the left are the goods avoiding lines while the graceful curves of the station roof complete an absorbing scene. *N W Skinner/ARPT*

The first batch of the second series of 'Derby Lightweight' vehicles consisted of 13 units that were earmarked for the modernisation of the West Cumberland lines, the first route to benefit from the new trains being the branch line from Carlisle to Silloth which was dieselised from 29th November 1954. These units were yellow diamond coupling code, this being a code used for units in the 79xxx series in the early days. The initial batches of units were built with full height windscreens which were soon modified with strengthening bars and later vehicles were constructed with these from new. The units comprised a Driving Motor Brake Second (DMBS) with 61 seats and a Driving Trailer Composite Lavatory (DTCL) with 9 first and 53 second class seats. This series of units, like their predecessors in West Yorkshire, had a relatively brief career and all had been taken out of service by the end of 1968. After the introduction of DMUs on the Silloth branch the Penrith to Workington route through the Lake District, and associated workings from Carlisle, were taken over by these units in early 1955. Here, a westbound train is depicted at Cockermouth station on 24th August 1963 on a beautiful section of line that was sadly closed to all traffic three years after this scene was recorded. *Roy Denison*

2nd- SINGLE	SINGLE -2nd
Blaenau Ffestiniog (North) to	Blaenau Ffestiniog (North) to
Blaenau Ffestiniog (North)	Blaenau Ffestiniog (North)
Roman Bridge	Roman Bridge
ROMAN BRIDGE	**ROMAN BRIDGE**
(M) 0/8 Fare 0/8 (M)	
For conditions see over	For conditions see over

Llandudno Junction was an outpost of the 'Derby Lightweight' units and in this portrait a couple of bystanders admire a passing train on the Blaenau Ffestiniog branch sometime in the early 1960s. The leading coach is a composite offering first class passengers the privilege of an uninterrupted view through the driver's windscreen provided, of course, he hadn't lowered the blind that gave a degree of privacy. *Online Transport Archive*

Derby-built 'lightweight' units (single cars)

A scene at Verney Junction station on 13th July 1964 showing the 5.57pm Buckingham to Bletchley train, formed of a 'Derby Lightweight' single car, pulling out of the station; note the ugly exhaust pipes. A small group of passengers wait for the unit to pass before crossing the tracks. The branch diverged from the cross-country Oxford to Cambridge line just west of Verney Junction station. Two vehicles of this type were built in 1956 specifically for use on the Bletchley to Buckingham and Banbury line; they were fitted with 150hp BUT (AEC) engines and weighed 27 tons. Vehicle No.M79900 had a small brake van and offered 61 second class seats while its sister unit, No.M79901, was constructed with a much larger brake van and consequently only had 52 seats. The units represented a brave attempt by BR to reduce operating costs on the branch and attract more passengers and they certainly achieved a dramatic turnaround in the line's fortunes, with a one third reduction in operating costs and a remarkable 400% increase in patronage. In view of this vastly improved financial performance, passengers must have been dismayed when the northern section of the branch from Buckingham to Banbury (Merton Street) was closed from 2nd January 1961 – the writing really was on the wall. The section as far as Buckingham survived until 5th September 1964 and it is to be regretted that a line relatively close to London should have been wiped off the railway map. The 'main line' from Oxford to Cambridge was also partially closed but at the time of writing it looks very likely that trains will, once again, run on this potentially very useful route. Note the sidings in the background which contain a rake of coaching stock and many wagons, including wooden-bodied specimens, loaded with coal. *Tommy Tomalin*

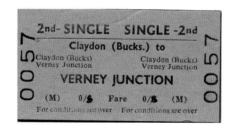

Derby-built 'heavyweight' units

Photographed on a cloudless spring day in 1966, a Derby-built DMU enters New Holland Town station with a service from Grimsby, the course of the line being indicated by the bracket signal just visible on the left of the shot in the far distance. The train would have continued to the Pier station to connect with the BR ferry across the Humber estuary. There was a triangle of lines here, the line on the right leading to Barton-on-Humber which could also be reached directly by trains from Grimsby along the bottom of the triangle, the tracks of which are just discernible. Today, Barton-on-Humber retains a regular service to and from Grimsby and Cleethorpes but virtually everything of railway interest in this picture has been lost following the commissioning of the Humber road bridge which immediately put paid to the ferry service. A total of 50 of these units was built at Derby between October 1956 and December 1957: they were the first DMUs to be delivered under the Modernisation Plan proper. Earlier units constructed at Derby had been manufactured using aluminium which had proved troublesome and costly, so the works opted for steel construction on a long frame. These units were heavier than their predecessors and became known as the 'Derby Heavyweight' units and all were initially based at Lincoln depot. The units were generally fitted with two 230hp BUT (Leyland) engines and had mechanical transmission except for one unit that had two 238hp Rolls Royce engines and hydraulic transmission. They were later refurbished and one or two lasted in service until 1992: some were extensively rebuilt as parcels cars. *David Mitchell*

Metropolitan-Cammell units

Metropolitan Cammell was the first private contractor to enter the field of DMU construction and the firm eventually built a total of 760 vehicles at its Washwood Heath, Birmingham, plant. The construction of the first batch of 36 units was on 'lightweight' principles, similar to the 'Derby Lightweight' design, and the first seven units were built specifically for the Bury to Bacup line in Lancashire and entered traffic in late 1955. The remaining, much larger, series of units was earmarked for use in East Anglia and the first went into traffic at Norwich (Thorpe) depot in January 1956. The units were equipped with two 150hp BUT (AEC) engines and the Driving Motor Brake Second (DMBS) coaches weighed 31 tons 10 cwt while the Driving Trailer Second Lavatory (DTSL) vehicles weighed 25 tons. It should be noted that there were variations in the seating capacity, the East Anglian units providing 128 second class seats whereas the Bury to Bacup units offered accommodation for 105 second class and 12 first class passengers. These units had the early standard yellow diamond coupling code and were later deemed to be non-standard, this leading to their early withdrawal and all had been taken out of traffic by the end of the 1960s. In this picture, taken on 3rd May 1959, a local train destined for Norwich is depicted running into Haughley station which served a small village and was located about three miles north of Stowmarket. Haughley was the point where the Bury St. Edmunds route diverges from main Ipswich to Norwich line, hence the bracket signal in the distance. Despite its modest status Haughley boasted a substantial station building and generous platform canopies and, of course, a signal box controlling the junction; the station lost its passenger service from 2nd January 1967. *R. C. Riley*

The initial batch of 36 units for the Bury to Bacup and East Anglian lines, which was numbered in the 79xxx series, was followed by many further BR orders, the last of which was for a batch of open second carriages with miniature buffets: these were delivered in May 1960. The earlier units had been constructed, as previously stated, as 'lightweight' vehicles, but the later units were of more robust build with a heavier and more durable integral body. The framework and roof panels were of light alloy while the steel body ends provided additional protection for the driver in the event of a collision. The later units had a mix of first and second class accommodation. The distinctive cab which made Metropolitan-Cammell units so easily distinguishable from other types was retained. The units were built in two-, three- and four-car formations and in the early years worked principally on the London Midland (LMR), North Eastern (NER) and Scottish Regions (ScR) but later in their careers they appeared on the Western Region (WR) whose diagrams took them across the regional border to the Southern Region (SR). So, it seems these units worked on all BR regions at some stage in their lives – quite an achievement. On the NER sizeable allocations were based at Bradford, Darlington and South Gosforth and in this delightful picture taken at Kildale, between Middlesbrough and Whitby, on sunny 18th June 1966 a party of walkers has just alighted from the train and is about to set off on a ramble. The rear unit also appears to be a Metropolitan Cammell-built example, but its leading vehicle has non-standard lining. *John Boyes/ARPT*

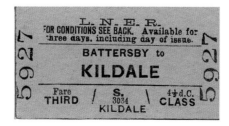

The station nameboard immediately identifies the location of this portrait but if it was not visible the towering structure in the background would have provided an immediate and unmistakable clue. Yes, it's Dalmeny, on the south bank of the Firth of Forth with the magnificent Forth bridge dominating the backdrop. A two-car local train, bound for Edinburgh Waverley, has just crossed the bridge and slows for its Dalmeny stop on 15th February 1965. During mid-1958 a fleet of 30 Metropolitan-Cammell units was allocated to Dundee and this unit is doubtless one of those. These low density units were undoubtedly one of the most successful and long-lived DMU classes and many were selected for refurbishment during the 1970s, these improvements including measures to reduce engine vibration, improve riding characteristics and better heating and lighting. A refurbished unit embarked on a three month tour of the United Kingdom to test the reaction of Passenger Transport Executives dedicated to improving public transport. Apart from a couple of single car 'heritage' units employed by Chiltern Railways, these units' longevity was emphasised when they became the very last fleet of first generation DMUs to be taken out of service at Longsight (Manchester) depot in late 2003. *John Boyes/ARPT*

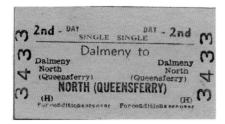

Cravens units

A scene at the now closed Peterborough East station on 26th June 1964 showing a Cravens two-car unit entering the station with a train from Ely. Cravens built 402 low density passenger-carrying DMU vehicles at their Sheffield works between 1956 and 1959 for use on all regions of BR except the Southern and Western. There were fleets of two- and three-car units originally but the centre cars in the latter were withdrawn in the 1968-70 period, thus converting them to two-car units. The fleet was distributed widely at depots as far flung as Crewe, Cambridge and Kittybrewster. The units were of all steel construction, including a fabricated underframe which incorporated a fuel tank. The most distinguishing feature of these units was probably the front end with two windscreens, very often with distinctive unpainted frames, providing excellent vision for the driver. Another interesting aspect of this stock was the use of BR Standard Mk.1 carriage components, such as doors and window frames so, viewed from the side, the vehicles could be mistaken for one of those coaches. The DMBS coaches had seating for 52 second class passengers while the DTCL coaches provided seats for 12 first and 51 second class passengers. Scheduled for early withdrawal the last units survived in passenger service until 1988 but some vehicles were converted for use in other guises such as route learning vehicles, parcels and sandite cars. Peterborough East station lasted until 6th June 1966 from which date all remaining services were concentrated on the city's other station formerly known as Peterborough North. *John Boyes/ARPT*

Birmingham RCW units

The Birmingham Railway Carriage & Wagon Co. constructed a total of 437 DMU carriages for BR, the most numerous being a series of 302 low density vehicles built for the LMR and NER over an almost two-year period from April 1957 to March 1959. The units were supplied in two-, three- and four car formations and all of the last-mentioned were initially allocated to the NER. The welded steel bodies were constructed on short underframes with glass fibre being used for the roof ends above the cabs. The formation of the three-car units was DMBS-TCL-DMCL, the motor coaches weighing 31 tons while the trailer cars weighed 24 tons; a total of 160 seats were available for the use of second class passengers while there were 24 seats for first class customers. The unit depicted in this photograph taken at Hornsea on 10th October 1964 appears to be a four-car formation and certainly a large proportion of those units was based at Hull Springhead depot. Those units were formed of a TSL and TBSL sandwiched between two DMCL vehicles and their total seating was 222 second and 24 first class seats. The three-car version of this type was particularly associated with two routes in the north-west of England, the lines radiating from Manchester to Blackpool and Buxton. Thirteen units employed on the first-mentioned line had their suspension modified to improve their riding characteristics and this was denoted by a wide white bodyside stripe which considerably brightened up their appearance. Buxton depot always took much pride in the appearance of their units which always seemed to be in particularly smart condition, this being emphasised by their white domes and red buffer beams. Sadly, it is no longer possible to reach Hornsea by rail; the branch from Hull fell victim to the infamous Beeching axe from 19th October 1964, just a few days after this shot was taken. *David Mitchell*

Gloucester RCW units

The Gloucester Railway Carriage & Wagon Co. (GRCW) constructed two batches of units, each batch consisting of 20 sets (40 vehicles). The DMBS vehicles, which were equipped with two 150hp AEC engines, weighed 30 tons 5 cwt and provided seats for 52 second class passengers. The DTCL coaches weighed 25 tons and accommodated 12 first and 54 second class passengers. The British Transport Commission (BTC) apparently approved a number of rolling stock orders, including an initial contract to purchase 20 GRCW units, at a meeting on 2nd December 1954 and the cost of each two-car unit was quoted as £33,568. The order was actually placed on 21st June 1956 with the units being earmarked for use on the ScR but in the event they were delivered to Longsight to cover for the late delivery of stock for a modernisation scheme in the Manchester area. Some of the units later moved to Scotland as per the original plan but others spent their entire lives on the LMR usually working from either Walsall (Ryecroft) or Longsight depots. A second order for a further 20 units was placed on 30th January 1957 and these were allocated to Leith Central depot for use on services in the Edinburgh area and it should be noted that the two batches were actually constructed concurrently between May 1957 and March 1958. During the 1960s when the Beeching Plan was being implemented many routes in Scotland suffered the loss of their passenger services and this naturally resulted in some units being declared surplus to requirements and moved to pastures new, being based at Cambridge for use on East Anglian lines. Withdrawals commenced in 1971 and the type slowly disappeared over a protracted period with the last surviving until the late 1980s; none was ever refurbished presumably due to the presence of asbestos. Vehicle Nos E51122 and E56300 were converted for use as the ER General Manager's saloon and renumbered DB975664 and DB975637 respectively, while a further two carriages were also renumbered in the departmental series for use as an ER inspection unit. A number of units were based at Walsall for employment on local services and in this picture one of these units is depicted at Birmingham New Street in 1965.
David Mitchell

English Electric 1,000hp Type 1 Bo-Bo

One of the unexplained mysteries of the BR Modernisation Plan concerns the plethora of Type 1 Bo-Bo designs that rolled off the production lines between 1957 and 1968. In June 1957 the first of the English Electric Co's Type 1 locomotives entered service, the forerunner of what subsequently proved to be one of the most durable and outstandingly successful designs built under the modernisation plan. Unfortunately, BR also placed orders for similar locomotives with other manufacturers and the machines produced by British Thomson-Houston, North British and Clayton all proved to be a total liability once they entered traffic and on average lasted about ten years in service and doubtless they spent much of that time out of service under repair. A number of the Clayton locomotives were withdrawn within five years of entering service – what an indictment! Political interference was alleged to have been a factor in the placing of orders at works located in areas of high unemployment. The English Electric locomotives were built in batches during a long period from their introduction in 1957 until February 1968 at their works in Newton-le-Willows, Lancashire and Robert Stephenson & Hawthorns, Darlington and were equipped with an EE Co. 8SVT 1,000hp engine. The locomotives generally weighed 72 tons, had four axle-hung nose-suspended traction motors and had a tractive effort of 42,000lb. The first 20 locomotives to be delivered were allocated to Devons Road (Bow) depot in East London for use on cross-London goods workings, this being a former steam shed that was extensively modernised and adapted to maintain BR's first fleet of main line diesel locomotives. The EE Co. Type 1s were based initially on the ER, LMR and ScR while a small number of the 1967/68 series was allocated to the NER. While the locomotives were very reliable in traffic there was criticism by some crews of the restricted visibility when working with the long bonnet leading (obviously they had not worked on steam locomotives!) and this was one of the factors that prompted construction of the so-called 'standard' centre cab Clayton Type 1 in 1962. This photograph shows No. D8028 at Inverbervie with the Branch Line Society/Stephenson Locomotive Society 'Scottish Rambler' rail tour on 22nd April 1962. Most of the motive power used on this tour was steam, including four of the ScR's vintage preserved locomotives, but No.D8028, which was based at Kittybrewster at the time, was used to take the participants along the Edzell and Inverbervie branches. *RCTS Archive*

A substantial number of English Electric Type 1s was based on the ScR so perhaps it is not entirely inappropriate that pictures of those locomotives on that region form the majority of the illustrations in this section. In the mid-1960s the bulk of this class in Scotland was allocated to either of the two principal Glasgow sheds, Eastfield and Polmadie, while there was a small number based at Inverness. Here, a most unusual combination of motive power is depicted with EE Co. Type 1 No.D8075 apparently waiting to leave Oban with a BRCW Type 2 pilot engine on an unrecorded date. No.D8075 was constructed by Robert Stephenson & Hawthorns at Darlington and entered traffic in July 1961. *RCTS Archive*

The modern factories in the background are typical of those that can be seen in any city in Great Britain and offer no clue to the location of this picture which was taken near Polmadie shed, Glasgow, in 1968. The locomotive seen here is No.D8122, one of those built by Robert Stephenson & Hawthorns, and it entered service in March 1962 at Polmadie. The first 128 locomotives were built with disc indicators while the remainder were constructed with four character headcode boxes. Note the recess beneath the cab window where single line tablet apparatus was fitted to those machines employed in areas where it was needed. *Eastbank Model Railway Club*

English Electric Type 1s were often used in pairs on Midland main line freight duties and in this shot Nos. 20 167 and 20 172 are seen passing Leicester on 9th October 1974. By the date of this photograph both of these locomotives had been in traffic for eight years and their paintwork was looking decidedly the worse for wear. *Chris Evans*

Brush 1,470hp Type 2 A1A-A1A

Unsung workhorses. A total of 263 Brush Type 2 A1A-A1A locomotives was out-shopped from the company's Loughborough works between October 1957 and October 1962. The first 20 locomotives were based on the Great Eastern (GE) lines at Stratford depot in east London and were equipped with 1,250hp Mirrlees, Bickerton & Day engines which powered four Brush traction motors. Later machines, comprising the vast bulk of the class, developed 1,365hp so were more powerful than the initial batch. The locomotives weighed 104 tons (with variations) and had a maximum tractive effort of 42,000lb and later in their careers the original power plants were replaced by English Electric 12SVT 1,470hp engines so the class had quite an eventful career. The class was launched into passenger service on 13th November 1957 when No.D5500 powered the 10.36am from Liverpool Street to Clacton and this locomotive apparently put in a workmanlike performance, accelerating smartly out of Liverpool Street and later breasting Brentwood bank at 38mph with a 302-ton train; it reached Shenfield 4 min. early. On the return run the only problem that arose concerned the temperamental train heating boiler which reportedly produced too much steam and proved tricky to control. By 1964 the entire complement of these locomotives was in traffic and confined exclusively to the ER with substantial fleets allocated to March, Tinsley and Wath depots while representatives could also be found at Finsbury Park, Ipswich and Stratford sheds. Later, Brush Type 2s considerably widened their horizons and could be found on the LMR and there was even a relatively small number of locomotives allocated to the WR. The locomotives were 'maids of all work' designed for mixed traffic use and this clearly included hauling colourful breakdown cranes as seen here at Doncaster in late 1966; unfortunately the identity of the locomotive is not known. The tracks of the East Coast Main Line are in the foreground while the background is dominated by the celebrated Doncaster Works which produced thoroughbreds such as the world famous *Mallard*. *David Mitchell*

It has to be said that the external condition of many BR diesel locomotives left much to be desired and in normal traffic conditions a thick coating of grime soon collected on the bodysides, harming BR's much vaunted 'modern image'. Proper, purpose-built maintenance facilities for diesel locomotives were distinctly lacking in the early years of the modernisation plan and many locomotives were serviced side by side with steam engines in sheds constructed in Victorian times – hardly an ideal situation. Tinsley diesel depot, however, was brand new and included a locomotive washing plant, from which Brush Type 2 No.5801 is seen emerging looking 'refreshed' after the luxury of a good clean. A wash and brush up, one might say!
Rail Photoprints

Whilst Brush Type 2 No.D5586 looks reasonably smart there is no doubt that the magnificent signal gantries, and collection of bracket signals in the background of this picture, really catch the eye and totally dominate the scene. Semaphore signals worked by manual signal boxes have been part of the railway scene since time immemorial and their rapid elimination is stripping the system of a lot of interest and character, though it has to be admitted that colour light signalling is safer and cheaper to operate. The distinctive building on the hill on the left is Alexandra Palace, which provides an instant clue to the location of this shot which shows a morning commuter train formed of non-corridor BR Standard coaches approaching Hornsey in April 1967. New in February 1960, No.D5586's first home was, appropriately, Hornsey where a fair number of these locomotives was based.
Rail Photoprints

Swindon-built 'Cross Country' units

Following the trend of doing things differently set by the Great Western Railway over a long period, the WR 'Cross Country' units were unique in being fitted with suspended gangways, screw link couplings and brackets for coach letters. The first unit was out-shopped from Swindon in late 1957 and all of the first series was allocated to either Cardiff Canton or Bristol, their principal sphere of activity being services from Birmingham Snow Hill to South Wales on which they were introduced on 10th March 1958. Powered by four 150hp AEC engines the units' formation was Driving Motor Second Lavatory, Trailer Second Lavatory Buffet and Driving Motor Brake Composite and the total seating capacity was 18 first class seats, 144 second including four in the buffet section. Whilst these units were undoubtedly very comfortable, it has to be said that provision for first class passengers clearly left something to be desired. They were marooned in two small saloons (one each for smokers and non smokers) at the outer end of the composite motor coach which would have been subjected to noise and vibration but, even worse, they had to walk through a second class saloon and negotiate a draughty large brake van to reach either a toilet or the buffet area. These units employed the same type of cab used on the earlier 'Inter City' DMUs constructed for the ScR's Glasgow to Edinburgh service but incorporated a destination indicator and four lamps so they didn't look quite so bare and functional. They were built in three distinct batches, the first series of 49 units entering traffic between March 1958 and March 1959 while the second batch of seven units was constructed specifically for the ScR's Aberdeen to Inverness route in late 1959. In 1961 a further series of nine units was built for the WR but the small buffet sections were omitted, presumably because they were uneconomic, and those units accommodated eight more second class passengers. The front end also incorporated a four character headcode panel so externally they were noticeably different to their predecessors. This photograph was taken at what remained of Barry Pier station on 13th April 1968, the coach nearest to the camera being a DMSL vehicle. Despite the premises' rather untidy appearance the station apparently remained open for occasional passenger traffic until 12th October 1971 but was officially closed in June 1976. *Online Transport Archive*

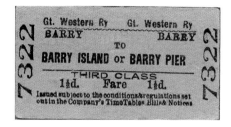

A small number of these units was constructed especially for use on the 108 miles-long Aberdeen to Inverness route, as previously mentioned, and were delivered to Kittybrewster shed between November 1959 and February 1960. They entered passenger service on 1st July and reduced the journey time between the two cities to an unprecedented 2½ hours with stops at only Keith Junction, Elgin, Forrres and Nairn. There were just two trains in each direction initially but such was the popularity of the new service that two additional services were provided from 12th June 1961 and all trains served Huntly in addition to the aforementioned stations without any increase in overall journey time. Here, a DMSL vehicle complete with 'speed whiskers' is nearest to the camera at a rather deserted Aberdeen station on 21st November 1963. *John Boyes/ARPT*

Above: The final series of 'Cross Country' units, as previously mentioned, did not incorporate a buffet area, and their front end design was also different to the previous batches due to the presence of a four character headcode panel. Little thought seems to have been given to the panel's design which looked very clumsy and hardly improved the units' appearance. In this photograph one of these later units, in woefully neglected condition, is seen leaving Templecombe on 5th March 1966 with a westbound working. The people on the station were probably railway enthusiasts mourning the Somerset and Dorset line which closed that weekend. *David Mitchell*

Opposite bottom: The former stone-built station at Elgin with its elegant columns was quite attractive and noteworthy because it apparently had two methods of platform lighting – note the fittings for both electric and gas. Note also the portable wooden steps provided for less nimble passengers. Routes used to fan out from Elgin to Lossiemouth, Cairnie Junction via Buckie and to Keith Junction via Craigellachie, but the first-mentioned lost its passenger service in 1964, while the other two routes were still operational when this shot was taken in April 1968 but lost their trains a few weeks later. This shot provides an excellent view of DMBC carriage No.Sc51781 with its very large brake van, two separate saloons for first class smokers and non-smokers, and rather cosy 16 seat saloon for second class travellers. Note the recess for tablet apparatus adjacent to the guards van doors, this being necessary because half of the route was single track. The vehicle depicted here was new in November 1959, lasted in traffic until March 1987, and was broken-up three months later. *Eastbank Model Railway Club*

British Thomson-Houston 800hp Type 1 Bo-Bo

Following the introduction of the English Electric Type 1s in mid-1957 a second Type 1 Bo-Bo design was formally delivered to BR at a ceremony at Euston station on 18th November 1957. The first batch of ten locomotives was supplied as part of the 'pilot scheme' to evaluate various designs, the principal contractor being British Thomson-Houston who supplied all of the electrical equipment. Various other companies were involved in the manufacture of these locomotives; the engines were a Paxman 16YHXL power unit, the bogies and main superstructure were built by the Clayton Equipment Co. while the underframe was built by the Yorkshire Engine Co. The last-mentioned company was also responsible for the final assembly and painting of the complete locomotives. The 800hp locomotives had a maximum tractive effort of 37,500lb and were capable of a top speed of 60mph though it is unlikely that this would be attained on a regular basis bearing in mind their intended use on slow moving, cross-London goods workings. The first ten examples were allocated to Devons Road (Bow) shed in east London and the final locomotive of this series entered service in November 1958. The class's relatively smooth entry into service apparently persuaded BR that the design was quite promising and, unfortunately, they then made the crucial mistake of ordering a further 34 machines before the type had been fully evaluated. These locomotives, built with BTH and the Clayton Engine Co. as the main contractors, entered traffic between October 1959 and February 1961 and were numbered D8210 to D8243. Problems with the engines arose after some time in everyday service and it became clear that the troublesome power plants required excessive maintenance. Furthermore, the type of short-haul goods working for which they were intended, like cross-London freights, was rapidly disappearing and these two factors precipitated the class's early withdrawal, the surviving examples being condemned *en masse* in March 1971. Four locomotives found a new lease of life in departmental use as carriage heating units, one of which, the former No.D8233, was eventually preserved. The first ten machines had a brief flirtation with Devons Road (Bow) shed, as previously mentioned, but later the entire class was concentrated on the ER at Finsbury Park, Ipswich, March and Stratford depots. Here, No.D8230 is depicted at Hornsey shed on 4th February 1967; this locomotive was new in July 1960 and lasted in traffic until the final survivors were withdrawn in March 1971 so it is arguable whether it was a good investment for BR.
Rail Photoprints

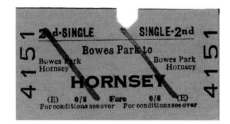

North British Locomotive Co 2,000hp 'Warship' Type 4 A1A-A1A

Some of the dubious locomotive designs produced under the Modernisation Plan, such as the BTH Type 1 Bo-Bos covered in the previous section, were perpetuated by BR with the result that they found themselves trying to operate the 'modern' railway with some very unpredictable diesel types. Mercifully, only five North British Locomotive Co. (NBL) Type 4 'Warship' Class A1A-A1A locomotives were constructed which was probably just as well as they were notoriously unreliable. The idea for these machines came from the V200 class diesel hydraulics operating in West Germany and BR awarded the contract to build five locomotives, reportedly at a cost of £87,500 each, to NBL which already had close ties with German locomotive manufacturers. The class was equipped with two MAN/NBL 12 cylinder L12V18/21A 1,000hp engines and each locomotive weighed 117 tons and possessed a maximum tractive effort of 50,000lb. The WR tended to do things differently and the locomotives had hydraulic transmission which was, of course, out of step with other BR regions who were adopting electric transmission as standard. In addition, they were one of the few main line diesel classes fitted with spoked wheels. It was, perhaps, tempting fate when the name *Active* was bestowed on No.D600, the first locomotive to enter service, perhaps the most inappropriate name ever given to a locomotive. *Active* was recorded, for example, as 'under repair' at Swindon Works on 3rd May 1959 and it was still present on 28th June. Later in its career No.D600 was repainted in corporate blue livery and became the only representative of its class to sport full yellow ends. During the early part of their careers these 'Warship' machines were entrusted with crack WR long distance express workings such as the prestigious 'Cornish Riviera Express', but towards the end they were based at Laira and largely confined to Cornwall where maintenance staff and enginemen alike were familiar with their fallibilities. It is unlikely that many of the local staff were in mourning when the entire class was unceremoniously withdrawn at the end of December 1967 and all of the locomotives were later broken-up at south Wales scrapyards. No.D603 *Conquest* was only eight months old when photographed heading an unidentified London-bound express at Hungerford on 4th July 1959. *R.C.Riley*

English Electric 2,000hp Type 4 1Co-Co1

English Electric 2,000hp 1Co-Co1 Type 4 No.D201 pauses at Grantham with an unidentified London-bound working, formed of Pullman cars, in April 1961. This locomotive was the second of its class to enter traffic, at Stratford shed in April 1958, but in May 1960 it was among the first locomotives to be transferred to the new diesel depot at Finsbury Park. No.D201 then spent some time employed on East Coast Main Line (ECML) expresses until the 'Deltics' established themselves on the route and No.D201 returned to Stratford in July 1961. Like so many sister locomotives, No.D201 finished its days on the former London Midland Region, based at Carlisle on unglamorous mixed traffic duties, surviving until the last full year of the class's operation being withdrawn in April 1984 so it had one of the longest periods of service of any member of its class. The author well remembers a journey behind the former No.D201 in September 1983 on a Yarmouth to Manchester Piccadilly holiday train that ran via Spalding and Lincoln – a far cry indeed from prestigious ECML expresses. *Tony Sullivan*

The ancestry of the English Electric (EE Co.) Type 4s can be traced back to two pre-nationalisation designs, Co-Co No.10000 which was introduced by the LMS in 1947, and the 'Southern's 1Co-Co1 locomotives Nos.10201/2 which emerged from Ashford Works in November 1950 and August 1951 respectively. No.10203 was a later, and more powerful, addition to the latter class which was built at Brighton Works and entered service in March 1954. The performance of these early diesel classes was a revelation compared to their steam counterparts and they were accumulating mileages double those of steam locomotives employed on similar work. When the modernisation plan was announced in 1955 BR decided to invite tenders for 174 'pilot scheme' locomotives of various power classifications to assess their capabilities and EE Co. put forward a 2,000hp 1Co-Co1 design employing a Mk.II version of the 16SVT engine already in use in No.10203 and ten machines were ordered for evaluation purposes. The proposed locomotives' external styling was largely based on that of No.10000 which resembled North American practice of the period. The chairman of the British Transport Commission was apparently unimpressed with the specification of the new design which he opined was insufficiently powerful to work heavy expresses and it was felt that if the locomotives were introduced on the Great Eastern line, for example, they would represent little improvement on the 'Britannia' Class steam locomotives they were intended to replace. The ER declined to accept a substantial allocation of the type but LMR operating authorities were keen to improve services on the West Coast Main Line (WCML) where the steam fleet was ageing so an order for a further 190 locomotives was agreed. Despite their reservations the first ten locomotives were allocated to the ER in 1958 with the rest being distributed among the LMR, NER and ScR, the first-mentioned region having the largest share. In this picture No.D332 is seen leaving Morecambe on 14th April 1963 after reversing with a Manchester to Glasgow train that had been diverted due to bridge repairs just north of Lancaster. Most EE Co. Type 4s had disc route indication but Nos. D325 to D344 had 'split boxes' displaying the train reporting number, as seen here, while later machines were fitted with a centrally placed headcode panel. No.D332 was one of a substantial number of these locomotives allocated to Crewe when new, in this particular case in February 1961, and it finished its career not far away at Wigan in March 1982. *Noel Machell*

A plaything for an EE Co.Type 4! A scene on Camden bank showing an immaculate No.D371 coming up the incline effortlessly with a short van train in tow on 11th August 1963. The locomotive is in particularly smart condition following its use on the Royal train which conveyed HM the Queen to the Royal Agricultural Show at Kenilworth on 4th July. Note the cables and small round plate on the nose end of the locomotive. These cables would be slung from the front cab of the locomotive back into the train to enable the travelling inspector to liaise with the Royal train staff. The London & Birmingham Railway obtained authorisation for a terminus at Camden Town in 1833 but decided that a terminus nearer London was desirable and a site at Euston Grove was agreed. Unfortunately, the extension involved crossing the Regent's Canal and it was not possible to avoid a 1 in 68/1 in 77 incline from the platform ends at Euston and for a time trains were cable-worked between there and the top of the bank. In steam days the ascent up to Camden presented a considerable obstacle particularly with a 'cold' engine and trains were often assisted up the short climb. *Rail Photoprints*

A down express with English Electric 1Co-Co1 No.D254 in charge emerges from one of the Kensal Green tunnels on 7th March 1964. Kensal Green station is located at the other end of the tunnels and is served only by trains on the local lines. No.D254, which entered traffic in December 1959 was an early casualty and one of the relatively few EE Co. Type 4s to be taken out of service in the 1970s, in this case in December 1977. *Rodney Lissenden*

One wonders how many enthusiasts have a picture of the Royal Train - those who wish to obtain one would certainly need to be 'in the know' and have impeccable sources of information. Here, No.D384 is seen passing Roade on 9th July 1964 hauling the Royal train which was conveying the late Queen Mother from London to the Royal show at Kenilworth. The photographer was certainly 'in the know' on this occasion being employed as a signalman at Roade and was no doubt issued with his personal copy of the 'top secret' special notice detailing the train's timings. What better source of information could one possibly want? It is recorded that the train was stabled overnight at Berkswell and a pair of specially cleaned Stanier Class 5MTs were used for carriage heating and as stand-by engines. The Royal train apparently spent some days in the area and on 12th July was taken from Stratford-upon-Avon to Windsor by 'Castle' Class 4-6-0 No.5063 *Earl Baldwin*, also no doubt specially cleaned. *Robin Patrick*

A classic Scottish scene. Scotland abounds with outstanding locations for railway photographers and the Forth bridge, Plockton on the Kyle line and County March summit on the West Highland line immediately spring to mind. None of those, however, offered the thrilling sight and sound of an English Electric Type 4 working on full power heaving a heavy express up a long, steep gradient but here is such a shot which depicts No.D236 climbing Beattock bank; this photograph was taken at Harthorpe on 1st August 1964. No.D236 was out-shopped from Vulcan Foundry in October 1959 and was initially allocated to Crewe North depot. It ended its career when it was condemned in January 1982 and was subsequently broken-up at Swindon in August of that year. *Rodney Lissenden*

A wet day at Garsdale. The Settle and Carlisle line's fickle, and sometimes downright inhospitable, climate is legendary and in this picture a diverted Glasgow to Birmingham express is seen passing through Garsdale station in pouring rain behind an unidentified English Electric Type 4 in March 1965. Let us hope that the locomotive's windscreen wipers were able to cope with the deluge. Note that the station has been kitted out with a full complement of station signs all painted in maroon, the LMR's regional colour. Garsdale used to be the junction for Hawes and Northallerton and, indeed, was the only passenger junction station on the Settle line. The last public passenger train ran to Northallerton in April 1954 while services to Hawes continued until March 1959. *David Mitchell*

2nd·SINGLE   SINGLE·2nd
Leeds to
Leeds   Leeds
Garsdale   Garsdale
GARSDALE
via Skipton
(N)   17/0   Fare   17/0   (N)
For conditions see over   For conditions see over

0109   0109

An up East Coast Main Line (ECML) goods working with No.D242 in charge is depicted near Deerness Valley signal box, about two miles south of Durham, on 20th May 1965. The signal box in the far distance, above the last vehicle in the train, is actually Relly Mill Junction, where the line from Blackhill converged with the ECML thus providing a direct run into Durham station; Deerness Valley box is out of sight behind the photographer. That box was located in a commanding position in the 'vee' of the East Coast and Bishop Auckland lines, the latter diverged from the ECML at Relly Mill, and Deerness Valley signal box's elevated location provided an excellent view of the trailing connection from the Blackhill line to the Bishop Auckland route and also access from both of those lines to the Waterhouses branch. The Bishop Auckland line is visible on the left of the picture but a connection from the Blackhill line to the ECML, which burrowed under the Bishop Auckland route, is just out of view. Services on the Blackhill line were withdrawn as long ago as May 1939 while those on the Waterhouses branch survived until 29th October 1951. Local passenger trains continued to run from Durham to Bishop Auckland until 4th May 1964, this being a very useful diversionary route along which Gresley Class A4 Pacifics could be seen hauling diverted ECML expresses. It should be noted that all of these routes were probably used by excursion workings after their official closure in connection with the Durham Miners' Gala Day. *Rail Photoprints*

The North Wales coast main line reverberated to the distinctive sound of the 16SVT engine for many years and was always a happy hunting ground for English Electric Type 4 aficionados. In this illustration taken in the mid-1960s No.D221 *Ivernia* has just left Llandudno with (what appears to be) a return excursion, probably heading for Manchester. The train is formed exclusively of LMS-designed rolling stock and the locomotive is carrying a paper reporting number on the front end to ensure it is correctly identified by staff. The bank of sidings to the left of the picture contains more rolling stock which would doubtless be forming later return trains from Llandudno. No.D221 was new in July 1959, named in March 1961, but was an unlucky machine being included in the first large batch of withdrawals in 1976 so its career was apparently cut short prematurely. *Tommy Tomalin*

The Penrith to Keswick/Workington line through the Lake District was one of the first routes in Great Britain to be worked by DMUs which took over the majority of local services in the mid-1950s. The line west of Keswick was sadly closed in 1966 and by 1967, with steam traction fast declining in the Carlisle area, the best hope for steam photographers were the Keswick Convention special workings which were locomotive-hauled through trains to and from London. On 15th July the inbound working produced a pair of Ivatt Class 4MT 2-6-0s, Nos.43121 and 43120, which had replaced BR Standard 'Britannia' Pacific No.70014 *Iron Duke* at Penrith. A week later, when the convention participants returned home, steam photographers were doubtless hoping for a similar combination of 'Ivatts' on the Keswick branch but must have been bitterly disappointed when English Electric Type 4 No.D313 was provided to pilot Ivatt 2-6-0 No.43139, the diesel later taking sole charge south of Penrith. The train is seen here leaving Keswick with a distant backdrop of Lake District fells. Note that parts of No.43139 have been cleaned, no doubt the work of enthusiasts who had hoped that the locomotive would pilot the diesel and not the other way round. Regrettably, the efforts of the steam photographers were almost completely wasted – you can't win them all! *Rail Photoprints*

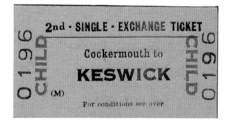

What a disgrace! No.40 052's supposedly green paintwork was extremely faded, and generally in shabby condition, when it was photographed at York hauling the 11.30am Poole to Newcastle train on 29th March 1975 - one wonders when it was last repainted. The adjacent Mk.1 compartment coach is in much smarter condition. No.40 052 entered traffic in December 1959 and was first allocated to York shed; it was withdrawn from Longsight in June 1983 and scrapped at Crewe in October 1983. *Chris Evans*

Railbuses

In the late 1950s BR's finances were in dire straits as a result of increasing costs and falling receipts and the economics of many rural branch lines in particular were under scrutiny, so in a last-ditch attempt to stave off closure it introduced a fleet of four wheel railbuses. Inexplicably, rather than standardise on one design, BR placed contracts for the construction of railbuses with no fewer than five different manufacturers, including Waggon and Maschinenbau of Donauworth, West Germany, and a total of 22 vehicles were built. The vehicle seen here was one of five, Nos.W79975 to W79979, constructed by Associated Commercial Cars of Thames Ditton, Surrey, in 1958 and No.W79979 underwent trials on the WR during that year before being taken into stock by the ScR. The remaining four vehicles, however, spent almost their entire working lives on the WR before being moved to the ScR in January 1967 where they lasted a further year before being taken out of traffic. These railbuses were powered by a BUT (AEC) 150hp engine, were 36 feet long over the body and weighed a mere 11 tons. They seated 23 second class passengers in each of the two saloons situated on either side of the luggage stowage space. This photograph was taken at Kemble on 1st February 1964 when the vehicle was being used on the Tetbury branch and it has to be said that BR really tried to save this short line by cutting costs and opening small halts adjacent to new housing development. A brave experiment, but it was all in vain as, regrettably, the increase in takings was insufficient to prevent closure which occurred from 6th April 1964. *Roy Denison*

Two railbuses, Nos.Sc79958 and Sc79959, were constructed by Bristol Commercial Vehicles, a subsidiary of the Bristol Aero Engine Company, using bodies built by Eastern Coach Works; the latter is depicted here in this picture taken at Perth motive power depot on 15th September 1963. No.Sc79959, which entered service at Leith Central in November 1958, incorporated a Gardner 6HLW six cylinder 112hp engine, weighed 13½ tons and was just over 42 feet in length. The passenger accommodation consisted of two second class saloons each seating 28 people, the saloons being separated by space for luggage and the entrance/exit doors. The vehicles, which represented the smallest class of railbuses numerically, were withdrawn from service in October 1966 and subsequently scrapped. *ARPT*

Another shot of a railbus at Perth shed, this time illustrating a vehicle manufactured by D Wickham Ltd of Hertfordshire who used a unique tubular body construction flexibly mounted on a tubular underframe. The railbus shown here is No.Sc79967, one of five in the Sc79965 to Sc79969 number series. The engine fitted to these vehicles was a Meadows 6 cylinder type 6HDT500 of 105hp and the vehicles seated 48 second class passengers, the internal layout being similar to that described above for the other two railbuses. The Wickham-built series of railbuses was the last to be delivered and also suffered comparatively early withdrawals, No.Sc79969, for example, entered traffic in July 1959 but was taken out of service in December 1963 so it must have had one of the shortest careers of any item of BR rolling stock. This picture was taken on 13th October 1963. *ARPT*

North British Locomotive Co 800hp Type 1 Bo-Bo

If there was a table of Modernisation Plan diesel locomotives showing BR's 'best buys' there is no doubt that the North British Locomotive Company's (NBL) Type 1s would not figure in the ratings. Actually, they would be near to the top of chart listing their 'worst buys' along with many other unsuccessful types constructed by the same firm. The class, which was intended for local freight duties, was evolved from the North British's earlier prototype No.10800 that was constructed in 1950. This incorporated a Davey Paxman 827hp RPHXL engine, which powered four British Thomson-Houston nose suspended traction motors, and weighed almost 70 tons. This machine was withdrawn in August 1959 but was retained by Brush Traction Ltd. for the development of traction equipment and not scrapped until May 1976. Ten of the ill-fated Type 1s, Nos. D8400 to D8409, were ordered as part of BR's 'pilot scheme', which initially involved the construction of 174 locomotives of various power classifications, and the NBL locomotives were purchased for evaluation against similar types being produced by both British Thomson-Houston and English Electric. The prototype used a Paxman engine and the new class employed the company's 16YHXL power plant which produced 800hp and powered four GEC traction motors. The locomotives weighed 68 tons, were 42ft 6ins. long and possessed a maximum speed of 60mph. Many BR diesel locomotives were plagued at that time with constant train heating faults but that was one defect from which the NBL Type 1 locomotives never suffered – they were not fitted with any train heating equipment. The class was out-shopped from NBL's Queens Park works between May and September 1958, its initial allocation being to Devons Road (Bow), Great Britain's first diesel locomotive maintenance depot. The locomotives were soon moved to nearby Stratford where they spent the rest of their short existence. Unfortunately, problems with the design quickly manifested themselves, especially inadequate ventilation which led to frequent engine seizures and another recurring defect concerned the non-standard control equipment which was prone to failure. The local goods duties for which the class was designed were dwindling and this, coupled with the class's unenviable reliability record, made it a prime candidate for elimination. When BR was reviewing the future of the entire diesel fleet it was, perhaps, inevitable that the NBL Type 1s would be earmarked for rapid withdrawal, no doubt to the annoyance of fitting staff at Stratford who earned enhanced overtime payments trying to sort out their problems. The North British Locomotive Company, which was formed in 1903 by the merger of three locomotive manufacturers in Glasgow, was one of the world's leading makers of steam locomotives and enjoyed an excellent reputation and even in the late 1950s had well over 2,500 staff on its payroll. The company had secured a contract with the German firm MAN to build diesel engines under licence but there were shortcomings in the NBL's work, its engines being less reliable than its German counterparts' products. North British had apparently sold diesel locomotives to BR at a loss in the hope of obtaining further orders and this, together with warranty claims on its failure-prone products, sealed its fate and NBL went into liquidation on 19th April 1962, a tragic end to a great organisation that had simply failed to adapt. In this portrait the doyen of this unfortunate class, No.D8400, is seen at Stratford depot in the early 1960s. *Rail Photoprints*

Parcels cars

Parcels car No.M55999, seen here passing Tipton on 30th July 1961, was the last of a small batch of three constructed by Cravens in mid-1958; the front end design provides an immediate clue to its origin. This vehicle entered service in August 1958 and was powered by two BUT (AEC) 150hp engines, weighed 30 tons and was 57ft 6ins. long. Originally intended for use on lines in Cumberland in multiple with 'Derby Lightweight' DMUs, when they were delivered it was decided that they were no longer required for such duties and the cars spent the greater part of their lives in the Manchester area. When this picture was taken No.M55999 was actually allocated to Stoke-on-Trent, while one of its sister cars was based miles away at Carlisle Upperby, but all three were congregated at Newton Heath towards the end of their careers. They were withdrawn in the early-1970s: this particular example succumbed in October 1973 and was broken-up in January 1975. *RCTS Archive*

Sporting a rather fancy gangway shield with 'speed whiskers' and horizontal lining to match the rest of the vehicle, parcels car No.W55991 is depicted at Subway Junction, near London's Paddington station, on 10th September 1960. This vehicle was one of ten constructed by the Gloucester Railway Carriage & Wagon Co. in 1960, six cars being earmarked for the WR while the remaining vehicles were based on the LMR. All of the cars were powered by two 230hp Leyland Albion 6-cylinder RE901 engines, were 64ft 6ins. long and weighed 40 tons (LMR vehicles) and 41 tons (WR vehicles); the number series was M55987 to W55996. The relatively high power of these vehicles ensured they could pull a trailing load if necessary. It should be noted that the WR cars were fitted with end gangways, as seen here, but their LMR sisters did not have gangways fitted. The vehicles had three sets of sliding doors on each side and the interior had straps for securing bicycles, hinged racks for small parcels, and letter racks. No.W55991 was based at Reading for many years but was eventually withdrawn from Cambridge depot in November 1990 and broken-up five months later. The profile of this otherwise rather obscure class was raised considerably during 1980 when one of the cars was used to haul material trains across Barmouth bridge at a time when locomotive-hauled trains were banned. *R.C. Riley*

BR/Sulzer 1,160hp Type 2 Bo-Bo

A grand total of 151 1,160hp BR/Sulzer Type 2 locomotives (later Class 24) was built, all being constructed by BR workshops at Crewe, Darlington and Derby; the number series was D5000 to D5150. The machines were powered by a Sulzer 6LDA28A engine and had four British Thomson-Houston traction motors. Interestingly, the first series of locomotives constructed were heavier than later batches and it seems there was a gradual reduction in the weight of the machines as the build continued. The first 114 locomotives numerically were fitted with train classification discs, but Nos D5114 to D5150, which were built at Derby, had roof mounted headcode boxes which radically altered their appearance and made them almost indistinguishable from their more powerful Class 25 descendants. The first 20 locomotives were supposed to be earmarked for the LMR but about 15 of those machines were placed on loan to the Southern Region (SR) as a stopgap due to the late delivery of its own fleet of BRCW Type 3 locomotives. The SR had cause to regret the late arrival of their stud of Type 3s because the BR/Sulzer Type 2s had a high axle load and their train heating boilers had to be removed before they could be used. In this portrait No.D5017 is depicted on 26th May 1959 at St. Mary Cray Junction, near Bromley, heading east with a freight train in tow. When this shot was taken the London to Dover/Ramsgate route was being improved in connection with the Kent Coast electrification and some sections in this area were being quadrupled, hence the presence of a trolley on the right of the photograph. *R. C. Riley*

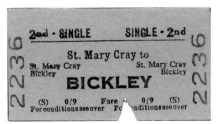

The sun may not be shining but, even so, BR/Sulzer Type 2 No.D5130 makes a fascinating sight at Garve while hauling the 10.40am Inverness to Kyle of Lochalsh on 24th May 1965. The train consists of six Mk.1 carriages, two vans and an observation car, quite a substantial load for a moderately powered locomotive, particularly bearing in mind the very stiff climbs on the Kyle line. Note the coal wagons in the goods yard, also the signal box and permanent way trolleys' storage shed, both of which are on the left of the picture. A connecting bus is just visible and one wonders where it was going – Ullapool, perhaps. *Noel Machell*

2729

2nd-SINGLE	SINGLE-2nd
Dingwall to	
Dingwall	Dingwall
Garve	Garve
GARVE	
(H) 3/3	Fare 3/3 (H)
For condit'ns see over	For condit'ns see over

2729

A large number of BR/Sulzer Type 2s were allocated to sheds in the London area with Finsbury Park and Willesden having the lion's share, while Cricklewood also had an allocation. In this portrait No.D5025 is depicted climbing Camden Bank with an unidentified working in August 1965. No.D5025 was built at Derby and entered traffic in October 1959 and lasted until withdrawn in January 1976; it was scrapped at Swindon works in July 1977. *Rail Photoprints*

A Bradford panorama. An unidentified BR/Sulzer Type 2 gives a 'Black Five' a helping hand up the 1 in 50 gradient from Bradford Exchange to Laisterdyke; the train is an express to King's Cross and this photograph was taken in July 1967. This combination would presumably have worked only as far as Leeds City where the train would have reversed and the two locomotives replaced by either a Brush Type 4 or 'Deltic'. The tracks on the extreme left served the local gas works (note the long lines of coal wagons) while those adjacent formed the Bradford avoiding line and converged with the Halifax route at Bowling. The five tracks on the right of the picture went to Bradford Exchange. *David Mitchell*

Photographed against the impressive backdrop of the hills of Snowdonia, No.D5140 approaches Morfa Mawddach with a southbound goods train in September 1967. The signal box which formerly controlled the junction with the Ruabon line is partially visible on the right, but by this date the latter route had been closed to passengers for almost three years and the rails may have been rather rusty. At the time of this picture goods traffic on the Cambrian lines appears to have been fairly buoyant and the train seen here has many empty coal wagons and a number of gunpowder vans in its consist. *Online Transport Archive*

BR/Sulzer 1,250hp Type 2 Bo-Bo

A pair of Type 2s, Nos.D7527 and D5291, head southwards through Harbury cutting with a long coal train in tow on 31st May 1966. The later series of these BR/Sulzer locomotives (which subsequently became Class 25 under TOPS) comprised 327 machines and they incorporated a 1,250hp 6LDA28-B power unit which made them marginally more powerful that their earlier sister engines (Class 24s). This series was constructed at BR workshops at Darlington and Derby while a small batch was produced by Beyer Peacock, an outside contractor. These locomotives could be observed at work on all BR regions, even the SR which did not have its own allocation. The earlier machines were equipped with gangway doors but these were not often used and later batches were built without them, thus giving a more attractive front end. *Robin Patrick*

When the perilous state of BR's finances came to the attention of staff in the Lancaster area they clearly recognised the revenue-raising potential of a toll bridge at Halton station. A farm track crossed the railway lines at this point and continued across the river Lune thus providing a link between the Lancaster to Settle road and Halton village. A penny to take a cycle over the bridge and threepence for a score of cattle may not sound much but, as they say, it all adds up and every little helps. One wonders if the tolls actually covered the crossing keeper's wages and whether any surplus cash was sent off to BR headquarters to reduce the deficit. Sadly, the Lancaster Green Ayre to Wennington line was closed from 3rd January 1966 and Morecambe to Leeds trains diverted via Carnforth. This shot, which dates from 26th May 1964, shows the 12.30pm Morecambe (Promenade) to Leeds train with BR/Sulzer Type 2 No.D5258 in charge. *Noel Machell*

A Morecambe to Leeds train, powered by an unidentified BR/Sulzer Type 2, rounds the curve at the approach to Clapham station in March 1966. The old Midland Railway signal box, just visible in the distance, was known as 'Clapham Junction' but, in the summer 1959 timetable at least, the station was listed as 'Clapham (Yorks)'. This location may not be quite as busy as its namesake in south London but its superb moorland backdrop is in a different class. The tracks to Ingleton, which go straight ahead, seem to be somewhat rusty and it is likely that this route, which lost its passenger trains in February 1954, had been closed completely by the date of this picture. *David Mitchell*

A BR/Sulzer Type 2 on Settle and Carlisle freight. No.D5204 comes round the curve from Rise Hill and approaches Dent station with a southbound goods train in tow on 29th March 1968. This route was almost entirely monopolised by diesels by the date of this photograph, steam servicing facilities having being withdrawn at Carlisle from the end of the previous year. There were, however, sporadic sorties by steam locomotives on ballast workings as far as Appleby but only enthusiasts with 'inside information' were likely to see them. *Noel Machell*

Despite the growth of continental holiday packages, in the early 1970s there were still many Britons who preferred a traditional 'bucket and spade' holiday at a resort and Great Yarmouth was a popular choice. That town was particularly favoured by people living in the West Midlands and in this shot BR/Sulzer Type 2 No.D7588 is captured passing Thetford with the 7.55am Walsall to Yarmouth holiday train on 4th September 1971. The moderately powered locomotive appears to be hauling a heavy train, quite a task for a single Type 2, so it was probably just as well there were no really steep gradients to be negotiated. *Terry Phillips*

One wonders how many of today's travellers speeding along the West Coast Main Line appreciate the vast amount of work required to excavate the very deep cutting at Roade. Needless to say when the route was being constructed in the mid-1830s there was no powered excavation equipment and everything had to be done by hand by teams of navvies, a truly laborious and backbreaking task. Problems digging the cutting and boring the nearby Kilsby tunnel caused a delay to the opening of the London and Birmingham Railway and it is recorded that, sadly, 26 men lost their lives during the tunnel works. The massive scale of the civil engineering operation at Roade can be appreciated from this picture of No.7512 leaving the cutting with the 11.13am Wolverton to Northampton Down Sidings goods working on 8th September 1971. *Robin Patrick*

Metropolitan Vickers 1,200hp Type 2 Co-Bo

A fleet of 20 Type 2 Co-Bo locomotives, Nos.D5700 to D5719, was ordered from the Metropolitan-Vickers Electrical Co. (Metro-Vick) as part of the British Transport Commission's 'pilot scheme' to evaluate various designs. The first machine to be delivered was No.D5700 and this arrived at Derby motive power depot in July 1958. The class, which was built at Metro-Vick's Bowesfield works at Stockton-on-Tees, incorporated a 1,200hp Crossley HST Vee 8 two-stroke diesel engine which was to provide a basis for comparison with the more conventional four-stroke engines being specified for other classes then being delivered. The locomotives, which were known initially as Class ML2 and intended for mixed traffic duties on the Midland lines, weighed 97 tons, were 56ft 7½ins long and possessed a top speed of 75mph. The peculiar Co-Bo wheel arrangement was reportedly used to enable an even distribution of weight on all five axles. On 1st October 1958 a pair of Metro-Vicks was put through its paces on a Hendon to Gushetfaulds (Glasgow) fitted freight working, which included a dynamometer car, and it was the intention to employ the class on the 'Condor' prototype freightliner service between the two yards when it was introduced in July 1959. The class's introduction into everyday service was marked by numerous and repeated failures, however, and steam locomotives quickly took over its rush-hour workings to Moorgate and those on the 'Condor'. The railway press ominously reported that in mid-January 1959 all of the fleet delivered by that time was congregated at Derby shed and had been temporarily taken out of traffic. By the middle of that year it had become clear that the class had serious, inherent problems and all 20 were once again out of service at either Derby or Cricklewood. In a desperate attempt to cure the class's defects, it was decided to send them to the maker's works at Dukinfield, near Manchester, for rectification and following this work they were allocated to Barrow shed, the entire class being officially based there by mid-1962. When a re-appraisal of BR's future motive power requirements took place in the late 1960s it was clear that these unsuccessful Type 2s would be first in the firing line and the class was quickly eliminated. No.D5701 is seen here at Hest Bank on a Barrow-in-Furness to Lancaster train on 13th May 1964. *Noel Machell*

Cynics might argue that the load of one parcels van was just about commensurate with the capacity of these unpredictable locomotives: No. D5717 is depicted at Carnforth with the 9.35am parcels train from Barrow-in-Furness on 20th May 1964. Perhaps the pinnacle of No.D5717's undistinguished career was reached when it was an exhibit at a freight transport exhibition at the Central Goods Station at Birmingham from 16th to 18th June 1959. No.D5717 had just been delivered and was no doubt in sparkling condition which impressed the gathered multitude. Well, after all, appearances can be deceptive!
Noel Machell

Two days after the previous shot was taken No.D5717 was still very busy and photographed at Silverdale in charge of the 9.53am Workington to Carnforth stopping train which took 3½ hrs. to complete the 81 miles-long journey. This was clearly a train designed for the most dedicated and patient traveller. Strangely, the front end of the locomotive appears to have been recently repainted but the rest of the bodywork is rather grubby. *Noel Machell*

Photographed on a rather gloomy day, an unidentified Metro-Vick Co-Bo is depicted entering Lakeside (Windermere) station with a train of five non-corridor coaches; this shot was taken in August 1964. Opened throughout in June 1869, this branch's heyday was probably prior to the First World War when day trippers flocked to Lake Windermere for a boat trip, there being little local traffic. The line was closed to passengers during the Second World War and by the time it reopened much of the holiday traffic had been lost to road transport. Passenger trains were withdrawn from 6th September 1965 and later plans to preserve the branch were thwarted by a road scheme but at least the section as far as Haverthwaite was saved. *David Mitchell*

Birmingham RCW 1,160hp Type 2 Bo-Bo

In the autumn of 1958 the first of a series of Birmingham Railway Carriage & Wagon Company (BRCW) Bo-Bo Type 2 locomotives was delivered to Hornsey depot for use on suburban services from King's Cross/Moorgate, the number series being D5300 to D5319. The locomotives were powered by a 1,160hp 6LDA28A Sulzer engine, weighed 77 tons 10 cwt and had four Crompton Parkinson traction motors. The new diesels reportedly took over operation of some Great Northern line (GN) suburban trains to and from Moorgate from 1st December 1958 with Nos.D5300/1/2/4/6 being noted in the first few days of the new arrangements. The machines had been undergoing trials along the GN main line at least as far as Newark where No.D5305 failed on 20th November and retired to the local shed where fitters, hopefully, diagnosed the fault but this incident clearly delayed its introduction into traffic. Another of the initial batch of these locomotives, No.D5303, was also an absentee from the Moorgate workings, being commandeered in December for trials over the Glasgow to Mallaig West Highland line which attains a height of 1,350 feet above sea level at Corrour. The Type 2 acquitted itself very well, taking 320 tons over this mountainous route which would have been well beyond the capacity of a Class 5MT steam locomotive which was limited to 250 tons unassisted. A further batch of these Type 2 locomotives, Nos.D5320 to D5346, was delivered to the ScR during 1959 and during the following year it was decided to concentrate all of the class in Scotland so the Type 2s use on the GN line was short-lived. In this picture No.D5319, the last of the GN locomotives to be delivered, in March 1959, is seen at Lairg on 26th May 1965 with the 10.30am Inverness to Wick train which included a mail coach marshalled immediately behind the locomotive. Part of the local Royal Mail van is just visible beyond the footbridge. *Noel Machell*

A pair of unidentified BRCW Type 2s leave Perth with an Inverness to Glasgow (Buchanan Street) train in August 1965. The long distance services that operated over the Highland main line at that time were heavy trains, hence the use of double-headed Type 2s over this very demanding route. Some trains divided at Perth with separate sections going to either Glasgow or Edinburgh and almost all conveyed a restaurant or buffet car. Note the tablet catcher on the locomotives, this being an indispensable piece of equipment for locomotives working the Highland lines. *David Mitchell*

2nd · SINGLE	SINGLE · 2nd
Dundee Tay Bridge	to
Dundee TayBridge	Dundee TayBridge
Perth	Perth
	PERTH	
	via Errol	
(H) 4/5	FARE	4/5 (H)
For condit'ns see over	For condit'ns see over

7006 7006

Birmingham RCW 1,250hp Type 2 Bo-Bo

Deliveries of the 1,160hp BRCW Type 2 locomotives continued until October 1959 when the final machine entered traffic but that was not the end of the story for these Type 2s. In June 1961 the first of a further batch of 69 locomotives, No.D5347, was delivered from BRCW's Smethwick works. This series of locomotives was equipped with an inter-cooled Sulzer 6LDA28-B power unit which developed 1,250hp and powered four GEC traction motors; the locomotives were geared for a maximum speed of 90mph. An interesting aspect of these locomotives was the considerable reduction of five tons in weight compared to the earlier machines. Externally, the principal difference between the two batches was the provision of roof mounted four digit headcode panels which radically altered the appearance of the front end; in addition the first 23 machines, Nos.D5347 to D5369, were destined for Eastfield (Glasgow) shed for use on the Highland lines and were fitted with recessed tablet catchers under the cab side window. Nos.D5370 to D5378 were earmarked for Thornaby shed, on Teeside, while the remainder, Nos.D5379 to D5415 were intended for use on the former Midland lines and were allocated to Cricklewood and Leicester depots. Here, No.D5387 is depicted taking a goods train through Stamford station, on the Peterborough to Leicester line, on 26th June 1964.
John Boyes/ARPT

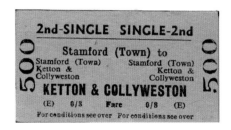

BRCW Type 2 No.D5361 approaches Banavie with a Mallaig to Glasgow (Queen Street) train on 9th October 1964. This locomotive was one of the batch of 23 ordered for use on the ScR and entered service in November 1961; it was withdrawn in January 1977, one of the very early withdrawals, and was cut up at BRFI's Glasgow works in April of the same year. Most of this later series of BRCW Type 2s survived until the mid-1980s so it seems that No.D5361 was a particularly unfortunate locomotive. *John Boyes/ARPT*

Deliveries of the BRCW Type 2s continued until October 1962 and No.D5413, seen here at Acton Wells Junction with a Cricklewood to Acton train of empty milk tank wagons, was one of the last to enter service. No.D5413 was later moved to Scotland where it was converted for pull-push working in November 1973; it was withdrawn from Inverness shed in April 1986. This picture was taken on 27th March 1968. *Robin Patrick*

Swindon-built 2,200hp 'Warship' Type 4 B-B

On 15th July 1958 the first Swindon-built 'Warship' B-B to enter traffic, No.D800 *Sir Brian Robertson*, made its public debut in passenger service when it powered the 'Cornish Riviera Express' from Paddington to Plymouth; the locomotive returned to London the following day hauling the 1.20pm Penzance to Paddington train. Based to a considerable degree on the German Federal Railway's (DB) 2,100hp V200 standard B-B class, the BR locomotives fell into three categories, the initial batch of three machines ordered as part of the Modernisation Plan 'pilot scheme', and the two separate production series batches constructed by Swindon Works and the North British Locomotive Company (NBL) which were different in many respects to their Swindon-built counterparts. The 'pilot scheme' 'Warship' locomotives weighed 78 tons and were powered by two Maybach Type MD650 12-cylinder engines which developed 1,056hp at 1,400rpm giving a total power output of just over 2,000hp. This power was transmitted to all four axles by a Maybach-Mekydro hydraulic transmission, this being a major departure from standard practice on other regions of BR where electric transmission was favoured. The main batch of locomotives produced at Swindon, Nos. D803 to D832 and D866 to D870, had two 1,152hp engines and were therefore marginally more powerful, producing more than 2,200hp. The locomotives' transmissions and bogies were largely identical to those of the DB locomotives but other components, such as the train heating boiler, were of British manufacture. The remarkable lightness of the design was due to the unique chassis which employed two solid drawn steel tubes threaded through a series of transverse plates. The NBL machines, Nos.D833 to D865, were slightly heavier and had two 1,100hp NBL/MAN 12 cylinder L12V18/21BS engines which gave a total of 2,200hp, with Voith hydraulic transmission. Unfortunately, the class's non-standard hydraulic transmission ensured that the 'Warships' did not stand the test of time, being earmarked for early withdrawal in common with other WR diesel hydraulic classes. An additional factor was undoubtedly the chronic unreliability of the MAN engines fitted to the NBL-built locomotives which were plagued by constant oil leaks. Some of the NBL-built series had a working life of less than eight years, an example being No.D848 *Sultan* which entered traffic in April 1961 and was withdrawn in March 1969 so it was hardly a worthwhile investment. The first 'Warship' to be taken out of service was No.D801 *Vanguard*, one of the three 'pilot scheme' machines, which was withdrawn in August 1968. In this shot one of the Swindon-built machines, No.D827 *Kelly*, is seen at Bodmin Road with (what appears to be) the 12.00 Penzance–Crewe train on 2nd May 1961. *Kelly* provided BR with a reasonable period of service, entering traffic in October 1960 and lasting until January 1972, that being the class's last year of service. *R. C. Riley*

Many passengers and enthusiasts probably feared the worst when it was announced that the Western Region was to take over control of all SR lines west of Salisbury (Wilton South) from 1st January 1963. One of the planks of BR's cost-saving programme at that time was the elimination or downgrading of supposedly 'duplicate' routes and it was unlikely that, against this background, the WR would choose to develop the 'rival' Salisbury to Exeter line in preference to its own route from Paddington to Exeter via Taunton. Various timetable alterations in the early 1960s had reduced the number of through portions conveyed by the 'Atlantic Coast Express' (ACE) so, to some degree, the decline had already started but much more drastic changes were yet to come. It was announced that from 7th September 1964 the principal Waterloo to Exeter service would be reduced to five weekday, diesel-hauled trains running to Exeter only and through portions to a plethora of small towns in Devon/Cornwall would cease. Perhaps the most controversial development was the WR's decision to replace the 'ACE', the busiest train of the day, with a train from Waterloo to Salisbury where passengers bound for the West Country would be required to change onto the Brighton to Exeter service. These developments were widely interpreted as the start of a deliberate policy of driving away as much traffic as possible from the former SR route in order to bolster the case for possible closure. It was decreed that the new traction on the former SR route was to be drawn from the WR's existing stud of 'Warship' B-B locomotives and the first reported appearance by a member of the class occurred in about mid-August when 'Warships' took over haulage of the up 'ACE'. The down 'ACE', however, apparently remained booked for steam until the end of the summer timetable. In this shot the up 'ACE', hauled by No.D816 *Eclipse*, is seen near Honiton tunnel on 3rd September 1964, just prior to the new timetable being introduced on the line. The WR had a reputation for over zealous application of acidic cleaning fluid which was not always sufficiently washed off with the result that the paintwork on many diesel locomotives suffered. The condition of No.D816 suggests that it may have been a victim of this problem. *David Mitchell*

Derby-built 'lightweight' units (later design)

The other Forth bridge. Photographed against the magnificent backdrop of the river Forth and distant Ochil hills, the driver of an Alloa to Grangemouth train hands over the single line token to the signalman at Throsk on 25th June 1966 having just passed over the 'other' Forth railway bridge. By the date of this photograph the service on this line consisted of only two rush hour trains in each direction on weekdays presumably for the benefit of work people. Predictably, the line was earmarked for closure, which occurred from 29th January 1968. The photographer deserves a commendation for taking this rare shot on this little known line apparently in preference to photographing steam traction, including Gresley Class A4 Pacifics, which could be seen a few miles away at Stirling. The unit seen here is one of the later series of Derby 'Lightweight' units which were introduced in May 1958. They were an updated version of the earlier 'Lightweight' units that appeared in April 1954 and had an improved cab and control system. The units were constructed mostly in two-car formations but three- and four-car units were also manufactured, the last mentioned series consisting of just six for the North Eastern Region. The DMBS vehicles were 58ft 1in. long, were powered by two 150hp engines and weighed 28 tons 10 cwt with variations; they generally had seating for 52 second class passengers. The DTCL carriages weighed 21 tons and offered 12 first class seats with accommodation for 53 second class passengers. It should be noted that a relatively small number of non-driving vehicles were also built and in some two-car units both vehicles were powered. The coaches were largely constructed of aluminium apart from the cabs, inner ends of the vehicles and headstocks. Derby works produced a huge number of DMU cars and in November 1959 No.M51562 became the 1,000th vehicle to roll off the production line; a ceremony took place to commemorate that historic landmark. The last of these units, which were very widely distributed across the BR network, was withdrawn from passenger use in 1993. *John Boyes/ARPT*

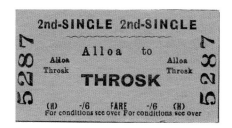

Gloucester RCW-built 'Cross Country' units

A total of 28 'Cross Country' units was constructed by the Gloucester Railway Carriage & Wagon Company between October 1958 and January 1960, most being 3-car units but there were three 2-car units that ran with Hawksworth locomotive-hauled composite coaches adapted to run as DMU trailers. The internal layout of these units was identical to the earlier Swindon-built 'Cross Country' units the first of which entered traffic in late 1957 but externally they were easily distinguished from those units by their 'Derby' cab which consisted of three windscreens whilst the distinctive Swindon units only had two. The DMBC coaches (37 tons) were noteworthy for their extremely large brake vans which occupied about a third of the vehicle while the remaining space consisted of two separate saloons accommodating 18 first and 16 second class passengers. The intermediate trailer TSLRB coaches (31 tons), known as Trailer Second Lavatory Buffet vehicles, offered 60 second class seats and had a tiny buffet area at one end of the coach with two lavatories at the opposite end. The DMSL vehicles (38 tons) had seating for 68 second class passengers arranged in three separate saloons with two lavatories located at the inner end of the coach. The motor coaches were powered by two BUT (AEC) 150hp six cylinder engines. The last of these units was withdrawn from service in the mid-1990s. In this photograph a train bound for Weymouth is depicted leaving Castle Cary on 6th October 1962 with the DMBC vehicle leading with Castle Cary's rather peculiar wartime signal box prominent in the background. It was built to replace an earlier box that fell victim to enemy bombing in September 1942 but was destined to have a relatively short life, being taken out of commission when Westbury panel box came on stream in 1984. The line to Dorchester was singled in May 1968 while the area once occupied by the neat goods yard has since been replaced by the inevitable car park. *R.C.Riley*

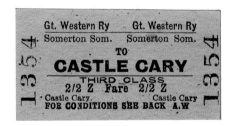

North British 1,000hp/1,100hp Type 2 Bo-Bo

Ten North British Locomotive Co. (NBL) Type 2 Bo-Bos, Nos.D6100 to D6109, were ordered for evaluation purposes as part of BR's 'pilot scheme'. The locomotives, which weighed 72 tons 10 cwt, were powered by a 1,000hp MAN engine which were built by NBL under licence from the German manufacturer. The transmission was electric, the locomotives being equipped with four GEC nose-suspended traction motors. Repeat orders were placed and the class eventually comprised a total of 58 locomotives. The first 38 machines were destined for the ER, being shared between Hornsey, Ipswich and Stratford sheds and No.D6100 made its debut on the Great Northern main line on 5th December 1958, being reportedly based at Newark for acceptance trials. On 12th December it was undergoing trials when it succumbed to failure, resulting in the locomotive and its eight-coach test train being rescued by a Class J11 steam locomotive of 1901 vintage! The initial batch of locomotives was to be based at Hornsey but deliveries were very slow and it was 10th April before No.D6101 was observed at Hornsey depot. The machines did not acquit themselves well during the test runs and other failures occurred with disturbing frequency, sometimes causing considerable delay to scheduled passenger workings. Deliveries continued, but it was becoming clear that the MAN engines were unreliable and suffering an unacceptable number of problems, including leaks and faults with the cooling system and within a year of the first deliveries a number of the locomotives were stored unserviceable at Peterborough. The final batch of 20 locomotives was sent to Kittybrewster shed, Aberdeen, as intended and perhaps this development prompted the decision to transfer all the ER machines to Eastfield shed, Glasgow, which was conveniently situated close to the NBL works where defects could, hopefully, be rectified. The ScR examples worked Glasgow to Aberdeen/Oban services and double-headed combinations were even entrusted with powering the Royal train from Aberdeen to Ballater. In the mid-1960s it was decided to fit new Paxman Ventura engines to 20 locomotives but withdrawals of the unmodified machines began in late 1967 and the locomotives with the Paxman engines only lasted four years longer. The locomotives were scrapped in Scotland not far from the works where they were built, the only exception being No.D6122 which found its way to Messrs. Woodham's yard at Barry, South Wales, where it lingered until June 1980. Here, an unidentified member of the class is seen powering a short freight in the delightful setting of Gleneagles station on 2nd July 1964. *Rodney Lissenden*

Photographed against an imposing background of splendid Scottish architecture, an unidentified NBL Type 2 is depicted leaving Fraserburgh in November 1964; note the locomotive is equipped with miniature snowploughs. On the right of the shot a DMU can be seen and perhaps that was employed on the short, 5 miles-long branch to St. Combs. The year 1964 proved to be the last full year that the Aberdeenshire fishing port of Fraserburgh was served by passenger trains, the branch service lasting until 3rd May 1965 while the main 47 miles-long route to Dyce Junction, just outside Aberdeen, was closed to passenger traffic on 4th October 1965. In the summer 1963 timetable six trains between Fraserburgh and Aberdeen were advertised in each direction on weekdays only. One of the intermediate stations, Mormond Halt, had what might be classified as an infrequent service with two northbound trains and one southbound train being scheduled to call on Saturdays only 'when required'. *RCTS Photo Archive*

Following their less than auspicious introduction on the ER all of these unpredictable machines were moved north of the border, as previously stated, and consequently all of the photographs covering the activities of this class were taken in Scotland. In this particularly interesting shot a pair of NBL Type 2s, Nos.D6141 and D6156, is seen climbing away from Aberdeen with a freight working in October 1965. Note the corridor connection between the two locomotives, this being one of the few pictures known to the author where the connection was in use and clearly visible. Southbound trains from Aberdeen face 7 miles of continuous climbing so the Type 2s would have had their work cut out with a heavy train. Railway photographers turning up at this classic location today would be bitterly disappointed to find that intrusive industrial development has taken place near the lighthouse. *Rail Photoprints*

One of the principal oversights of the BR modernisation programme was the lack of suitable maintenance and servicing facilities for diesel locomotives and BR's critics would have needed to look no further than Fort William shed which had apparently become a forgotten outpost. The dereliction and decay are almost unbelievable but, presumably, staff were expected to undertake basic servicing in the roofless old steam shed. The NBL Type 2s were notorious for persistent oil leaks and presumably the large cans were part of the shed's emergency supply. Note that part of the ground appears to be covered in oil – surely not all of it could have escaped from a Type 2. If the staff at Fort William needed to send a defective locomotive away for rectification there was no need to worry because Eastfield shed was only 123 miles down the line! *Allan Trotter/Eastbank Model Railway Club*

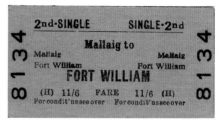

Dust to dust, ashes to ashes. While the performance of the NBL Type 2s may have been a persistent headache for the ScR's maintenance and operating departments, the class provided a bonanza for the local scrap dealers who were probably starting to run out of work as the steam fleet declined. Many of the unfortunate NBL Type 2s were broken-up at J. McWilliam's yard which was situated in Shettleston, Glasgow, almost within sight of the NBL factory where they had been constructed, in some cases less than ten years previously. In this picture taken at the yard in mid-1968 Nos. D6139 and D6150 await their fate against a back-ground of piles of twisted scrap metal. The distinctive NBL diamond shaped makers' plates removed from steam locomotives were always sought after by collectors but one wonders whether there would have been much demand for those seen here! *Allan Trotter/ Eastbank Model Railway Club*

North British 1,100hp Type 2 B-B

A total of 58 Type 2 B-Bs, Nos.D6300 to D6357, was constructed by NBL over a four year period from late 1958 to November 1962. The locomotives could reasonably be described as being equivalent to half of the same manufacturer's Type 4 'Warship' A1A-A1A design that was introduced in January 1958 because they were fitted with one MAN 12 cylinder L12V18/21S power unit rather than two. It should be noted, however, whereas the initial batch of six 'pilot scheme' B-B machines was fitted with the same 1,000hp engine as the 'Warships' the bulk of the class was equipped with an uprated version which developed 1,100hp. The 'pilot scheme' locomotives were heavier than the main series, weighing 68 tons in contrast to the production series which weighed 65 tons. Hydraulic transmission, which was much favoured by the WR, was the Voith/NBL LT306r version. These machines were troublesome from the start and, despite their manifest fallibilities, BR rashly placed bulk orders at a time when they were suffering considerable loss of both passenger and freight business and rapid dieselisation was seen as the railway's saviour. Many locomotives were placed in store after only six years of active service and it is likely that a large proportion were actually inactive during that time, receiving attention on shed. The first withdrawal occurred in December 1967, just five years since the last example went into traffic and a small contingent theoretically remained in traffic until January 1972. The class was an appalling investment for the British taxpayer so perhaps it is just as well every locomotive was scrapped, none surviving as a tangible reminder of that fact. Some diesel classes may indeed have been the railway's saviour but certainly not this class of unsuccessful NBL Type 2s! No.D6327 is depicted at Ilfracombe on 22nd July 1964. *R.C.Riley*

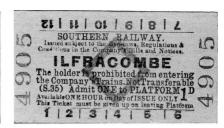

English Electric 1,100hp 'Baby Deltic' Type 2 Bo-Bo

In May 1959 Hornsey depot took delivery of No.D5900, the first of a series of English Electric Co. (EE Co.) 1,100hp Type 2 Bo-Bos which were intended for use on cross-London freights over the Widened Lines towards Farringdon. The locomotives were equipped with a nine cylinder Napier Deltic T9-29 engine which powered four EE Co. traction motors, and they weighed 74 tons and had a top speed of 75mph. The engine was a smaller version of that fitted to the prototype 'Deltic' and the Type 2's shape was also similar to that locomotive so the class became universally known as the 'Baby Deltics'. Unfortunately when the first locomotive was delivered to BR it was found to be overweight, a major culprit being the train heating system generators but other components, which were heavier than anticipated, also contributed to this problem. Efforts were made to reduce the weight of the locomotives by replacing steel fittings with aluminium where possible, but the machines were still too heavy for the Widened Lines so they were put to work on King's Cross to Cambridge expresses instead. During their first few years in traffic depot staff were working overtime trying to overcome various problems, initially with ancillary equipment, and later the engines were plagued with recurring faults. It was reported that up to October 1960 the locomotives had only achieved an average of 50,000 miles in traffic and 44 engine changes had been necessary in 18 months and this on a fleet of only ten locomotives. In late-1962 the patience of the ER operating authorities finally ran out and locomotives that failed were banished to the dump at Stratford, nine being reported as being stored unserviceable in February 1963. A modification programme was initiated no doubt with the intention of curing the class's long list of problems and the refurbished locomotives emerged in two tone green livery with four character headcode panels having replaced their original discs and communicating end doors. Unfortunately, while the locomotives really looked the part of a 'Baby Deltic' and were more reliable, such a small class remained vulnerable to policy changes and when the National Traction Plan was drawn up in the late 1960s the EE Type 2s were an obvious target for elimination. Withdrawals commenced in September 1968 and the last of the class was taken out of traffic in March 1971. English Electric produced some of BR's finest diesel classes but the 'Baby Deltics' were not among them and will be remembered for all the wrong reasons. The excessive exhaust fumes emitted by these locomotives are exemplified here in this portrait of No.D5904 leaving King's Cross station with empty Pullman carriages in the mid-1960s. The locomotive had been refurbished by this time and is not in original condition. *Rail Photoprints*

Swindon-built 'Inter-City' units

In April 1959 Swindon Works produced the first of 21 three-car units (plus some spare vehicles) for use on the services from Glasgow to Ayrshire, the units being similar in many respects to the 'Inter City' DMUs constructed in 1956/57 for use on the Glasgow to Edinburgh via Falkirk route and the WR's Birmingham to Swansea service. The latter units had been the first DMUs to be constructed on 63ft 5in. underframes. Like their predecessors the Ayrshire units incorporated two different designs of driving motor coach, one of a standard type with a full width cab while the vehicle at the opposite end had a very small cab and a corridor connection which enabled two three-car units to be coupled together to form a six-car rake with a gangway throughout the whole formation. The carriage (DMBSL) with the standard arrangement of a full width cab had seating for 52 second class passengers while the vehicle at the other end (DMSL) provided 64 second class seats. These units were among the most interesting in the BR fleet and even had two different types of intermediate trailer coaches! Ten of the carriages were trailer first vehicles (TFK) with 42 seats while the remaining eleven were composite coaches (TCL) with seating for 18 first class passengers and 32 second class, so the units with TFK coaches had a very high proportion of first class accommodation. Both types were compartment vehicles and each had lavatories at opposite ends of the carriage. In August 1973 vehicle No.Sc51011 was damaged beyond repair as a result of a fire at Kinning Park and replaced by former 'Inter-City' coach No.Sc79168 which was new in April 1957. In this picture a DMSL carriage, with its corridor connection prominent, is the leading vehicle of this train which is depicted at Girvan in the 1970s. *The late Derek Cross*

The principal job of the Swindon-built three-car DMUs used on the Ayrshire services was to provide a fairly intensive service between Glasgow and Ayr but the units also worked through to Stranraer. There were still flecks of snow in the gullies when this portrait was taken near Pinmore, also in the 1970s. The intermediate coach is a trailer composite (TCL) and, in contrast to the other vehicles, its roof had recently been repainted suggesting that the vehicles were 'shopped' individually and not as a unit. The distinctive 'Swindon' cab will be noted which, while not aesthetically pleasing, was certainly more attractive than the clumsy BR gangway shield seen in the previous illustration. *The late Derek Cross*

Derby-built St Pancras–Bedford units

The scene is just south of Derby Midland station on 24th May 1959. Apart, possibly, from a few specks of dust on the roof, this 4-car DMU is in absolutely immaculate condition so perhaps this photograph was taken during its initial venture into the outside world. The unit was one of 30 constructed at Derby for the St. Pancras to Bedford service and records reveal that the first unit was released from shops in May 1959 so this was obviously one of the first of its type to see the light of day. These high density units were powered by four 238hp Rolls Royce engines and the stock had hydraulic transmission. The units consisted of two Driving Motor Brake Second coaches, one Trailer Second and a Trailer Second Lavatory seating a total of 352 second class passengers (later reduced to 348). It is, perhaps, surprising that neither first class accommodation was provided bearing in mind some of the quite affluent middle class areas through which the units operated, nor toilet facilities in each coach. The first units reportedly arrived at Cricklewood depot on 14th May 1959 and they were put through their paces on test trips to iron out any problems prior to entering traffic. The big day came on 28th September 1959 when the units entered revenue-earning service for the first time, initially on steam timings. Their introduction into traffic presumably went fairly smoothly because it was decided to oust steam traction entirely and convert the complete service to DMU operation from 11th January 1960 but that is when the problems started. During the first two weeks of the new service many units suffered teething troubles, no doubt a result of very intensive diagramming, and steam traction had to be reinstated on at least three morning rush hour trains from Bedford and, presumably, their corresponding return workings. Later the service improved considerably, this being reflected in vastly increased ticket sales at many stations some of which boasted a remarkable upsurge of 25% in receipts. The cost of introducing the new trains, including the investment in a brand new depot at Cricklewood, was said to be £2.5m. *R.C. Riley*

BR/Sulzer 2,300hp/2,500hp Type 4 1Co-Co1

The first 2,300hp BR/Sulzer 1Co-Co1 Type 4 locomotive, No.D1 *Scafell Pike*, was out-shopped by Derby Works in May 1959 and after some weeks trial running it entered service in August 1959 at Crewe North shed pending the completion of diesel servicing facilities at Camden. The first ten machines were equipped with the Sulzer 12LDA28 2,300hp twelve cylinder engine which were supplied from that company's Winterthur works in Switzerland. The locomotives, which weighed 138 tons 2 cwt, were designed to haul 660 tons on level track at 74mph, and had a maximum speed of 90mph. The Sulzer

engine was based on a similar design supplied to continental railways before the Second World War and had a first class record which prompted many repeat orders; the engine on the Type 4 powered six Crompton Parkinson traction motors. The overall design of the locomotives owed much to the LMS-designed Co-Cos Nos.10000 and 10001 but the bogies were basically a copy of those used on the Bulleid SR 1Co-Co1 diesel locomotives. The 2,300hp 'Peaks' were quickly ousted from WCML passenger work by English Electric Type 4s and spent much of their life working coal trains from Toton to Whitemoor yard. Here, No.D1 is depicted approaching Peterborough with one such working on 13th February 1971. This locomotive survived until October 1976, the last member of the class being taken out of traffic in late 1980. Perhaps the legacy of the first ten 'Peaks' was their appealing name, the main production run being always referred to in the same way despite the fact that almost all of those that carried names were named after regiments! *Terry Phillips*

The 10.25am Leeds (City) to Glasgow (St. Enoch) train, with No.D24 in charge, speeds through Garsdale on 1st March 1963. In times gone by Garsdale was known as Hawes Junction where passengers could change for Hawes and the line along Wensleydale; changing trains there on a wild, windswept night must have been quite an experience. The route east of Hawes closed in April 1954 but the short connection from Garsdale to Hawes survived with a very meagre passenger service until it, too, succumbed from 16th March 1959. Garsdale, where the Midland Railway built 16 cottages for staff, was something of a social centre for the isolated railway community, the tank house being used as a village hall for many years while the down platform waiting room doubled as a chapel where the vicar of Garsdale held monthly services. *Noel Machell*

When the first series of ten BR/Sulzer Type 4s entered traffic the LMR was already contemplating the introduction of the main production series with an improved power rating of 2,500hp for which the Crompton Parkinson traction generator, that was fitted to the earlier batch, had adequate spare capacity. The generator was said at the time to be the largest so far employed in Europe. The first of the main series to be delivered, No.D11, entered traffic initially at Camden but soon found its way to Derby shed to where the bulk of the class were subsequently delivered, thus beginning a very long association with the Midland main line. This batch of 2,500hp locomotives was easily distinguishable from their earlier counterparts by their split headcode boxes which replaced the steam age headcode discs employed on the first series but centrally positioned four-digit headcode boxes were fitted to later locomotives. A total of 193 'Peaks' was eventually constructed but it should be borne in mind that Nos.D138 to D193 employed Brush traction motors rather than Crompton Parkinson. Unfortunately the Midland main line rarely attracted photographers so consequently no photographs of 'Peaks' on that route were submitted for publication in this album but here is a shot of a member of the class on a Liverpool to Newcastle-upon-Tyne train. The locomotive is No.D76 and this illustration shows it threading Marsh Lane cutting on the short climb from Leeds to Cross Gates; this picture was taken in June 1967. No.D76 was new in November 1960 and continued in service until November 1983 but it remained more or less intact until it was scrapped at Crewe in November 1988. *David Mitchell*

Contrary to popular belief the S&C line is not always being buffeted by strong winds or lashed by driving rain and when the landscape is bathed in sunshine it is incomparable, at least in the author's opinion. Here, BR Sulzer Type 4 No.D28 is seen coasting downhill at Helwith Bridge with the southbound 'Waverley' on 3rd June 1963. A line of wagons can just be discerned on the extreme left of the picture, these being stabled on a goods line serving the Ribblesdale Lime Company's works which formed a triangle with the main line. The layout there was controlled from Selside signal box, which was opposite the triangle on the 'up' side of the main line, and is partially visible in the distance. The chimneys marking the location of Horton-in-Ribblesdale quarry are on the horizon in the background. Cows and sheep in the fields and the river Ribble complete this classic Pennine scene. *Noel Machell*

The principal production series of BR/Sulzer Type 4s was closely identified with the Settle and Carlisle line for more than 25 years from 12th June 1961 when they were first rostered to haul the 'Thames-Clyde Express', replacing Gresley Class A3 Pacifics. They also appeared occasionally on the Leeds to Glasgow expresses and the 'Waverley' from that date but from 3rd July both services were regularly powered by 'Peaks', no doubt to the frustration of steam aficionados. In this picture No.D107 is seen just north of Horton-in-Ribblesdale station heading to Carlisle with the 'Thames-Clyde Express' on a beautifully sunny 3rd June 1963; the station building is just visible in the background. This machine was out-shopped from Crewe in June 1961 and was allocated to Derby shed like so many others of the class; it was taken out of service in March 1987 so had quite a reasonable innings.
Noel Machell

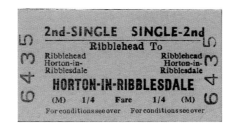

The down 'Thames-Clyde Express', headed by BR/Sulzer Type 4 1Co-Co1 No.D12, passes the remains of Newlay and Horsforth station, in the Leeds suburbs, in June 1967. The station closed its doors for the last time on 22nd March 1965. The fast tracks on the right of the picture are out of use. This locomotive was one of the very few (Nos. D11 to D15) that had the four-character headcode boxes but also the gangway doors. *David Mitchell*

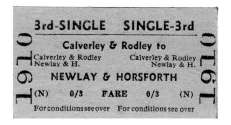

Pressed Steel 3-car suburban units

Springtime on the Berks and Hants route. An idyllic scene at Little Bedwyn on 12th April 1963, with an attractive little church in the background and the Kennet and Avon canal running beside the railway tracks in the foreground. The lock gates appear, superficially at least, to have seen better days and one wonders whether the canal was navigable to this point at that time. The peace and tranquillity is momentarily disturbed as a 3-car Pressed Steel DMU forming an eastbound working rushes past, after leaving Bedwyn station which is a mile or so away behind the photographer. A total of 42 of these high density units was built by Pressed Steel, which was part of the British Motor Corporation, for WR suburban services from London Paddington, the first appearing in November 1959. They had 64ft-long bodies and were powered by four BUT (Leyland) 150hp six cylinder diesel engines. These units consisted of a Driving Motor Brake Second (65 seats), a Trailer Composite Lavatory (originally 24 first and 50 second class seats) and a Driving Motor Second (originally 91 second class seats). It should be noted that the units were not built with gangways between vehicles, but following public pressure it was decided to fit them, which gave all passengers access to a lavatory. This work, which was completed by 1972, resulted in a marginal loss of both first and second class seats. The units were displaced by more modern stock in 1992 but migrated to other areas where they survived, amazingly, until the early months of the 21st century so they were exceptionally long-lived units and many subsequently survived into preservation.
Tommy Tomalin

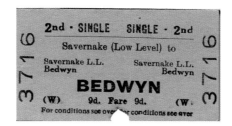

Birmingham RCW 1,550hp Type 3 Bo-Bo

The Southern Region's (SR) fleet of Type 3 Bo-Bos was undoubtedly one of the success stories of BR's Modernisation Plan and was an integral part of the SR's operations for many years. Built at the Birmingham Railway Carriage & Wagon Company's Smethwick factory, the first locomotive of the class made its debut on the SR at Hither Green on 17th December 1959. The locomotives were delivered much later than anticipated and less powerful BR/Sulzer Type 2s from the LMR had been deputising on various duties. The Type 3s were fitted with an eight-cylinder 1,550hp Sulzer 8LDA28 engine which provided power to the main Crompton Parkinson generator while the traction motors were manufactured by the same company. The locomotives weighed 73 tons 8 cwt and had wheels of 3ft 7in. diameter. It should be noted that 12 locomotives, Nos. D6586 to D6597, were built with narrower bodies for use on the Hastings line. The BRCW Type 3s were the first main line diesel locomotives fitted with electric train heating, were dual braked and also had the distinctive SR indicator blinds. When this picture of No.D6546 heading a down goods train at Paddock Wood was taken in 1961 the locomotive was almost brand new, judging by its pristine condition. The station was being modernised for the forthcoming Kent Coast Electrification and was a hive of activity: note the newly raised platform, concrete mixer and recently laid conductor rails. On the right of the shot a new 2-HAP electric unit is berthed prior to entering traffic. *ARPT*

7 | 8 | 9 | 10 | 11 | 12

British Transport Commission (S)

PADDOCK WOOD

5918

PLATFORM TICKET 2d.
Available one hour on day of issue only.
Not valid in trains. Not transferable.
To be given up when leaving platform.
For conditions see over

1 | 2 | 3 | 4 | 5 | 6

This viewpoint at the eastern end of Southampton Central station has attracted many generations of photographers and in this portrait BRCW Type 3 Bo-Bo No.D6523 is depicted approaching the platforms on 4th August 1964 with a train of oil tank wagons, doubtless destined for Fawley. The remains of a connection into the docks which used to cross the road can be seen in the centre of the picture. *Rail Photoprints*

A large number of BRCW Type 3s were based at Eastleigh so it is appropriate that a picture of one of the class at that location is included in this selection of photographs. Here, No.D6549 takes a lengthy freight train past Eastleigh on 3rd April 1965; the consist appears to include many oil tank wagons towards the rear of the train. The tracks on the right provide access to the shed while in the background the motor coach of a 'Hampshire' DEMU can be seen. New in April 1961, No.D6549 lasted in service until it was withdrawn in February 1989. *Noel Machell*

An unidentified BRCW Type 3, hauling a train of 3-TC/4-TC units, enters Brockenhurst station with the 9.30am Waterloo to Bournemouth some time in September 1966. This route was being electrified at this time and was in a transition period with an incredible hotchpotch of steam, diesel, electro-diesel and electric traction; it is likely that this train had only recently been booked for a BRCW Type 3 in preference to steam traction. Electric working had not yet started at Brockenhurst, note the rusty conductor rail, but the SR was anxious to replace steam traction on as many services as possible using Type 3s as a stopgap measure hauling non-powered 4-TC units which were eventually to form the majority of Bournemouth Line services with high powered electric units. Whilst the Bournemouth electrification brought a vast improvement in terms of frequency and reduced journey times the travelling public was less than impressed with the 'new' stock which was largely converted Mk.1 loco-hauled carriages. The austere style of the units and their thin, hard seating came in for criticism while the 'monastic blue' livery with its unattractive egg-shell finish did nothing to enhance the appeal of the stock. *ARPT*

A gentleman unloads the boot of his car apparently oblivious to BRCW Type 3 No.D6554 passing in charge of a goods train; it is likely that the locomotive was making a lot of noise as it attempted to gain momentum before the start of the steep climb towards Bincombe tunnel. This photograph was taken on 20th August 1967 six weeks after the end of steam on the 'Southern'. The railway installations at Weymouth have, sadly, contracted over the years partly as a result of changes to traditional 'bucket and spade' family holidays as more people took cheap overseas trips, and the growth of private motoring. In times past Weymouth struggled to cope during the peak summer months with Channel Islands boat trains heading for the quay and hordes of holiday-makers taking advantage of the town's sandy beaches. There used to be large banks of carriage sidings and, of course, a sizeable steam motive power depot which latterly had a substantial allocation of Bulleid Pacifics. *Noel Machell*

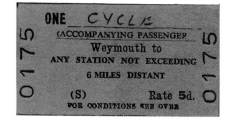

The first BRCW Type 3s to be delivered were based at Hither Green depot in the south-east London suburbs and for a period in the early 1960s the entire class was shedded there for duties on the SR's South Eastern and Central divisions. In late 1962 a small number of locomotives was transferred to Eastleigh, a trend that continued and by late 1964 a considerable number was based at that shed; by that time the Hastings-gauge Type 3s had moved to St. Leonards. Later still, the Type 3 machines really spread their wings and were put to work on Portsmouth to Cardiff trains and those from the Welsh capital to Chester and North Wales. Complex cyclic diagrams ensured that the locomotives returned to Eastleigh for maintenance every three days – well, at least in theory! In the author's experience photographs of operations in the eastern part of Kent are hard to find so it is likely that this picture of Dumpton Park on 13th July 1968 with No.D6560 entering the station is quite rare. The locomotive was powering the 12.20pm Ramsgate to Wolverhampton train while the 10.10am Victoria to Ramsgate, formed of the inevitable 4-CEP units, is on the down line. The gas lighting suggests that this station dated from Victorian times but actually Dumpton Park station was a very late newcomer to the railway network, dating from 1926 when the enterprising Southern Railway built this section of line in order to concentrate traffic on a new station in Ramsgate which replaced two wholly inadequate pre-grouping terminals. *Terry Phillips*

Swindon-built 'Trans-Pennine' six-car units

Ironically, one of the smallest DMU fleets, the 'Trans-Pennine' units, probably had the highest profile of any type of diesel unit. Eight six-car units plus three spare vehicles were constructed at Swindon Works in 1960/61 for the arduous Liverpool to Leeds/Hull line across the Pennines and they entered traffic amid a fanfare of BR publicity on 2nd January 1961. The units consisted of two Driving Motor Composite coaches (21 first and 36 second class seats), two Motor Brake Second vehicles (48 second class seats), a Trailer Second Lavatory (64 second class seats) and a Trailer First Lavatory Buffet carriage (18 first class seats plus 8 seats in the buffet section). The capacity of each six-car unit was 60 first and 232 second class seats plus eight in the buffet, thus giving a total seating capacity of precisely 300. There were heavy gradients on the line across the Pennines, such as the 7 miles-long climb at 1 in 96/105 from Huddersfield to Marsden, and in order to provide sufficient power these units incorporated two non-driving power cars which made them unique among the numerous and varied BR DMU fleets. The units were powered by eight 6 cylinder 230hp Leyland/Albion EN.902 engines supplied by British United Traction Ltd thus giving a total output of 1,840hp. The units benefited from work by a design consultant and the internal appointments were quite attractive, the first class compartments being favoured with sapele mahogany panelling, walnut grey partitions, grey curtains and dark blue upholstery of patterned moquette. It is fair to say that the new stock revolutionised services between the Mersey and Humber areas with a more generous timetable and reductions in journey time of more than 40 minutes; the use of 'Trans-Pennine' head boards and roof boards probably gave the service a special identity. Unfortunately, the appeal of the service was eroded when the M62 motorway was brought into use in the 1970s and in 1975 it was further downgraded when buffet facilities were withdrawn. Even worse, was the use of other DMU vehicles at times of low availability of 'Trans-Pennine' carriages. This picture shows the striking front end of a 'Trans-Pennine' unit at Neville Hill depot on 5th May 1963. *John Boyes/ARPT*

Photographed against a wild and rugged Pennine backdrop, a Leeds to Liverpool train is depicted near Marsden on 23rd April 1962. Alas, the train is not displaying a headboard but at least some of the intermediate carriages appear to be carrying 'Trans-Pennine' roof boards. The stylish front end, made of fibreglass, was one of the innovations suggested by industrial design expert E.G.Wilkes; this was considered a major step forward when compared to the drab and uninspiring front end of the earlier Swindon 'Inter City' units. During 1977 the 'Trans-Pennine' fleet was merged with surplus Western Region 1963-built 'Inter-City' units working from Manchester to Hull and Cleethorpes via Sheffield along the Hope Valley line. They also worked from Hull to York, and when BR abandoned through Nottingham to Glasgow trains via the Settle and Carlisle line the hybrid units were diagrammed to work from Leeds to Lancaster, thus providing a connection for passengers travelling from the West Riding to Scotland. Despite these encouraging developments the fleet's decline started in 1981 and vehicles needing heavy expenditure were sidelined. The replacement of the units on the Hope Valley services was planned from 13th May 1984 but many had been kept going with string and a prayer and two loco-hauled diagrams had to be introduced earlier than anticipated simply because there were insufficient serviceable units to operate the service. Apart from one train on 14th May 1984 from Cleethorpes to Doncaster the last booked workings occurred on 13th May and the units faded into history. Regrettably, no vehicles of either type were preserved possibly due to the prohibitive cost of removing blue asbestos contamination, a great pity bearing in mind they were arguably the most luxurious first generation DMUs produced under the Modernisation Plan. *Noel Machell*

English Electric 1,750hp Type 3 Co-Co

The driver of English Electric (EE Co.) Type 3 Co-Co No.D6853 seems to be taking a lot of interest in the photographer's camera as his goods train approaches Fishguard and Goodwick station on 15th August 1963. His locomotive had only been in traffic for a few weeks, its official release date being July 1963, and it was initially allocated to Landore depot at Swansea, one of the major diesel maintenance sheds in south Wales. Steam traction was being rapidly eliminated in this part of Wales at the time – two grimy locomotives can be seen sitting on Goodwick shed. This Type 3 class, which originally totalled 309 machines, is still in everyday service on the National system at the time of writing and must rank as one of the most successful, possibly the most successful, produced as part of the BR Modernisation Plan. These 1,750hp locomotives, which were built over an almost six year period from December 1960 to November 1965, are powered by an English Electric twelve-cylinder 12CSVT power unit which provides current to six EE Co. traction motors. The locomotives have a maximum speed of 90mph, weigh 103 tons with variations, and their similarity with the same manufacturer's Type 4 machine will be noted but the Type 3s were shorter, lighter and had a better power/weight ratio. The first locomotives entered service at Stratford shed in east London and could be found on express workings from Liverpool Street but generally the type was not associated with such high profile employment being the backbone of mundane day in, day out mineral workings especially in South Wales and the north-east of England.
Noel Machell

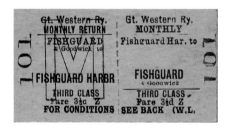

Operating practices on Britain's railways have changed beyond recognition over the last 50 years and the type of train depicted here, an unfitted coal working with a brake van at the rear and the locomotive propelling a diesel brake tender, has long since passed into history. Diesel brake tenders were introduced to enhance the braking force on unfitted or partially fitted goods trains and were often propelled by the locomotive hauling the train, as seen here. The locomotive depicted is No.D6772 and this portrait was taken near West Hartlepool on 15th May 1965. *Rail Photoprints*

The English Electric Type 3s will always be associated with the movement of heavy freight trains throughout the industrial areas of south Wales and in the mid-1960s about half of the class was allocated to depots in that region. Here, No.D6916 is seen at Radyr on 18th August 1966. Note the DMU hauling two vans on an adjacent track. *Online Transport Archive*

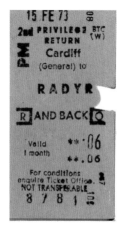

The county of Lincolnshire has never attracted many railway photographers who were perhaps deterred by its mainly flat landscape, so the author was particularly pleased when this shot of No.D6716 leaving Spalding was submitted: unfortunately the precise identity of the train is not known. No.D6716 was allocated to Stratford depot when new in June 1961 and was presumably still based there when this shot was taken on a rather hazy 9th September 1967. Once a relatively busy rail centre, Spalding suffered the loss of its through London services in October 1970 when the East Lincolnshire line was partially closed. The link from Spalding to Peterborough was shut at the same time but was later re-opened following the intervention of the local authority, and the line is still very much in business at the time of writing. *Tommy Tomalin*

Snowy Stockton. English Electric Type 3 No.D6897 leaves Stockton-on-Tees station with an unidentified working on 9th February 1969. The Type 3 is piloting a Brush Type 4 which was presumably ailing or, perhaps, had succumbed to total failure. No.D6897 was one of a number of these machines built by Robert Stephenson & Hawthorns Ltd. at Darlington and this particular locomotive entered service in April 1964. Sadly, since this portrait was taken the station seen here has undergone drastic 'rationalisation', the overall roof has gone and the track layout has been considerably simplified. *Rail Photoprints*

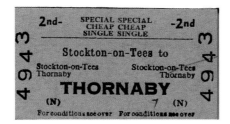

English Electric 3,300hp 'Deltic' Type 5 Co-Co

Few classes of diesel locomotive captured the imagination of diesel enthusiasts as much as the Type 5 3,300hp 'Deltics' which seemed to be the very embodiment of power, progress and, of course, speed. Their distinctive drone and imaginative two-tone green livery also added to their undoubted appeal. These Co-Co locomotives, which were built by the English Electric Co. at Vulcan Foundry, Newton-le-Willows, Lancashire, were modelled on the prototype 'Deltic' that had accumulated 400,000 miles in ordinary BR service since it took to the rails in October 1955. The production series machines comprised a class of 22 locomotives, each being equipped with two 18-cylinder Napier 'Deltic' engines developing 1,650hp. The locomotives weighed 99 tons in full working order, were 69 feet 6 ins long and had fuel tanks with a total capacity of 900 gallons. The greater part of their lives was spent hauling the fastest and most prestigious expresses on the East Coast Main Line and when they entered service eight locomotives were based on both the Eastern and Scottish Regions with six on the North Eastern Region. When the winter timetable came into force on 11th September 1961 the introduction of the 'Deltics' facilitated remarkable reductions in some schedules with, in some cases, savings of 59 minutes being reported. In the second year of the class's operation, after the usual initial teething problems had been ironed out, 88½ per cent availability was being recorded. Here, No.D9007 *Pinza* is seen passing Holloway South Down signal box with a northbound Pullman working on 9th June 1963. Apart from the brake vehicles at each end of the train the formation is made up of Metropolitan Cammell Pullman carriages that may have ridden better than their older counterparts but certainly lacked the appeal of traditional, opulent Pullman travel. *Rodney Lissenden*

York is the location of this illustration which shows 'Deltic' Type 5 No.D9020 *Nimbus* heading past the engine shed (behind the photographer) and towards the station; this picture was taken on 4th October 1964. *Nimbus* had the shortest career of any of the class, having entered traffic in February 1962, and it was one of the first two 'Deltics' to be taken out of traffic in January 1980 – a dubious distinction indeed. *David Mitchell*

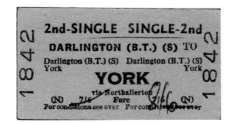

Nimbus is seen again, this time awaiting departure from King's Cross station with an unidentified express; this shot was taken on 24th May 1965. While steam enthusiasts doubtless mourned the loss of 55 Gresley Pacifics that were supposedly displaced by the 'Deltics', diesel aficionados were spellbound by the unmistakable drone emitted by the locomotives, their shiny bodywork and constant blue haze exhaust. The author well remembers travelling on the very last ordinary 'Deltic' working into King's Cross, on New Year's Eve 1981, hauled by No.55 015 *Tulyar* which was greeted by hundreds of adoring fans. Somehow King's Cross station would never be quite the same again. *ARPT*

The East Coast Main Line may be ideal for passengers in a hurry but from the enthusiast's point of view it is largely flat and featureless. Some of the more interesting stretches of the route are in Northumberland where the line runs close to the North Sea and in this splendid photograph an unidentified 'Deltic' (possibly No.D9003 *Meld*) is seen approaching Alnmouth on 21st May 1966. The train is mainly comprised of stock in maroon livery but coaches were being repainted in BR's corporate blue and grey colours at that time and three examples are visible in the train's formation. The village of Alnmouth takes its name from its geographical location at the mouth of the river Aln and part of the village can just be seen in the middle background while the North Sea dominates the horizon. *David Mitchell*

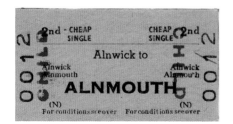

A London-bound express rushes through Doncaster station behind Type 5 'Deltic' No.D9021 *Argyll and Sutherland Highlander* on 3rd June 1966. The majority of the 'Deltics' entered service in 1961 the only exceptions being Nos.D9020 and D9021 which were introduced in February and May 1962 respectively. No.D9021 was initially based at Haymarket shed, Edinburgh, and ended its career at York where all the remaining members of the class were congregated towards the end. Withdrawal came in December 1981 and *Argyll and Sutherland Highlander* was broken-up at Doncaster Works in August 1982. *Robin Patrick*

Beyer Peacock 1,700hp 'Hymek' Type 3 B-B

Widely considered to be one of the most aesthetically pleasing designs produced under the BR Modernisation Plan, the first Beyer Peacock 'Hymek' Type 3 B-B, No.D7000, was handed over to the WR at a short ceremony at Paddington station on 16th May 1961. The preliminary order for 45 of these locomotives was placed by the British Transport Commission (BTC) in June 1959 and just over a year later the order was increased to 95 machines, all of which were to be constructed at Beyer Peacock's Gorton, Manchester, works. The order was further increased by six machines a little later thus bringing the total number of locomotives ordered up to 101. When the class entered traffic it was the intention that it would be principally used to replace steam traction on general purpose work in the Bristol area, the west of England and South Wales, including services to and from the Capital. These 1,700hp locomotives were powered by a Bristol Siddeley/Maybach MD.870 engine and employed a K.184.U Stone-Maybach Mekydro hydraulic transmission; the control equipment was supplied by the Brush Electrical Engineering Co. Ltd. The locomotives were 51ft 8½in. long, weighed 74 tons and had a maximum speed of 90mph; the bogies were of the cast steel Commonwealth type. The BTC's Design Panel and its various consultants played a significant role in the styling of the locomotives, a priority being the need for 'clean lines and keeping the body as free as possible of extraneous detail'. The class's pleasing appearance is exemplified in this view of No.D7033 posing at Llanelly with the 7.45am Fishguard Harbour to Paddington on 17th August 1963. In the 1961 summer timetable the equivalent train left Fishguard at 7.50am and its advertised arrival time at Paddington was 3.10pm on Mondays to Fridays, and 3.20pm on Saturdays; the train conveyed a restaurant car from Swansea. No doubt these timings were for steam motive power and the use of diesel traction considerably reduced the journey time. *Noel Machell*

Undoubtedly one of the most fascinating routes worked by the 'Hymeks' was the obscure 56¼ miles-long secondary line from Carmarthen to Aberystwyth in west Wales. This route served some of the Principality's most remote rural communities such as Lampeter and Tregaron, but apart from those small towns the line was hardly fertile territory for the railway. The 1960 summer timetable listed a basic service of three daily trains in each direction on weekdays only, plus a Saturday only express from Swansea to Pwllheli and back during the height of the season for the benefit of holiday-makers heading for the holiday camp at Pwllheli. The passenger service on this little-known line was scheduled to be withdrawn from 22nd February 1965 but the section between Strata Florida and Aberystwyth was abandoned prematurely from 14th December 1964 due to flooding. Here, the 11.55am Aberystwyth to Carmarthen train is depicted at Trawscoed on 14th July 1964 with 'Hymek' No.D7030 in charge. This station was one of those that lost its passenger trains prematurely as a result of the floods. *David Mitchell*

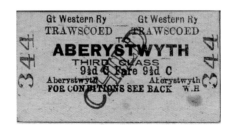

London's Paddington station is the unmistakable location for this illustration which shows No.D7076 awaiting departure with an unidentified working on 30th July 1964. New in May 1963, No.D7076 was initially allocated to Old Oak Common shed and, following its withdrawal in May 1973 after exactly ten years in service, was transferred to departmental use at the Railway Technical Centre at Derby. A further ten years elapsed before it was acquired by a group based at the East Lancashire Railway so its future is now assured. *Rail Photoprints*

2nd · SINGLE   SINGLE · 2nd
Southall to
Southall   Southall
Paddington   Paddington
PADDINGTON
(W)   1/11   Fare 1/11   (W)
For conditions see over For conditions see over

27008300083
27000083300083

Birmingham RCW 'Calder Valley' units

A fleet of 30 three-car DMUs was ordered by BR from the Birmingham Railway Carriage & Wagon Co. with a view to replacing steam traction on the Calder Valley main line which links Manchester with the West Riding via Todmorden. The line carried long distance passenger services including those serving Liverpool in the west and Harrogate/York in the east and there were some quite lengthy journey times. Unusually, it was decided to locate the first class seating behind the driver in both motor coaches rather than a trailer vehicle which would not have been subject to as much vibration and noise, but at least passengers had the attraction of a forward view through the driver's window. The units consisted of two motor coaches, the Driving Motor Brake Composite seating 12 first and 33 second class passengers while the other motor vehicle was a Driving Motor Composite Lavatory with 12 first and 54 second class seats: the intermediate Trailer Second Lavatory car provided 72 seats. The units had considerable affinity with the same manufacturer's earlier designs of DMU constructed in the late 1950s for the London Midland (LMR) and North Eastern (NER) regions which eventually totalled 302 vehicles in a variety of formations. Each power car of the Calder Valley units, which were of all steel construction, was powered by two Rolls Royce C6-N FLH130D 180hp engines which gave them a very high power/weight ratio, this being essential in view of the very heavy gradients on this cross Pennine route. The units were ordered in two separate series, the first order for 20 units for the NER was placed in April 1959 while the second order was for 10 units for the LMR. Strangely, the LMR's batch was more lavish and had, for example, Brazilian zebrano wood veneer panelling in the first class whereas passengers using the superior accommodation on NER's units had to make do with plastic laminates! The Achilles's heel of this stock was its propensity to catch fire, apparently due to design faults with the exhaust system and heating ducting, and in 1963 a particularly serious incident occurred when a unit caught fire in Sowerby Bridge tunnel, fortunately without any loss of life. Later in their career these units became a familiar sight at locations such as Blackpool, Sheffield and Hull and there was even a diagram that took one to Cambridge via the 'joint' line from Gainsborough to March. The vast majority of the units were refurbished but they were slowly withdrawn during the late 1980s and all had gone by the end of 1990. Here, a Calder Valley unit coupled to a Metro-Cammell set, is seen at Laisterdyke, between Bradford and Leeds; the two tracks on the extreme left served the local gas works sidings while the two immediately adjacent tracks, to the left of the bridge pier, formed the Bradford avoiding line to Bowling Junction. The units were probably working a Manchester (Victoria) to Leeds service and this picture was taken in June 1967. *David Mitchell*

Brush 2,700hp Prototype 'Falcon' Type 4 Co-Co

In the early 1960s a number of experimental locomotives were placed on loan to BR by various manufacturers and put through their paces on 'road tests' in different parts of the system. One of Brush Traction's contributions was Type 4 2,800hp No.D0280 *Falcon*, the largest and most powerful locomotive the company had ever produced, which was out-shopped in October 1961 and allocated to Finsbury Park depot. This machine weighed 115 tons, was 65 feet long over its buffer beams, had a fuel tank capacity of 1,400 gallons and was capable of 100mph. The locomotive was powered by two Bristol-Siddeley Maybach MD655 engines each producing 1,440hp at 1,500 revolutions per minute. *Falcon* was used on some very demanding tests and reportedly hauled, and restarted, 20 coach trains on the 1 in 37 Lickey incline and 17 coach trains on the notorious Dainton bank in Devon; it also achieved 100mph on several occasions. BR was clearly impressed with No.D0280 and purchased the locomotive in December 1970 when it was re-numbered 1200. *Falcon* lasted until October 1975 when it was taken out of traffic at Ebbw Junction shed and subsequently broken-up at Cashmore's Newport scrap yard in March 1976. Interest in diesel classes among enthusiasts was in its infancy at that time; if No.D0280 had survived a little longer there would no doubt have been people clamouring to save it from the scrap man's torch. Bristol Temple Meads station is the setting for this shot of *Falcon* at the head of an unidentified passenger train in April 1967. The attractive *Falcon* insignia is visible on the bodyside and for reasons that are not immediately clear the locomotive's cab area had obviously been cleaned recently but not the rest of the body panelling. Note the soot encrusted station roof, a legacy of the steam age. *Rail Photoprints*

BR/Maybach 2,700hp 'Western' Type 4 C-C

Subway Junction, near London's Paddington station, is the location of this portrait which shows No.D1035 *Western Yeoman* in charge of an unidentified express on 19th October 1963. Arguably the most popular diesel class ever built for use on BR, a total of 74 Type 4 C-C 'Westerns' were constructed, shared between Swindon (Nos. D1000 to D1029) and Crewe (Nos. D1030 to D1073). The 2,700hp locomotives, which weighed 108 tons, were powered by two 12 cylinder Maybach MD655 V12 65 litre engines, each producing 1,350hp and the hydraulic transmission used was the Voith/North British L630rV type. In the mid-1950s the BTC appointed the London-based Design Research Unit to advise on rolling stock design and the new ideas proposed by this organisation are thought to have influenced the class's final design and resulted in one of the most pleasing and stylish locomotive types produced under the Modernisation Plan. The fleet was ordered in September 1959 and the first locomotive started trial running on the WR in late 1961. Unfortunately, soon after test running commenced various bogie faults became apparent and an 80mph speed restriction was temporarily imposed on the class. Further problems developed with the Maybach engines, which had been manufactured under licence in Great Britain, and it appears that sub-standard materials were used, this being the direct cause of many failures. The WR managers were unable to reach agreement on the livery to be used on the 'Westerns' and a poll was conducted among the general public and, surprisingly, maroon was the most favoured colour and subsequently applied to the vast majority of the class. No.D1000 *Western Enterprise*, however, was out-shopped in an experimental fawn/grey colour which became universally known as 'desert sand', while another example appeared in 'golden ochre'. The class qualifies for inclusion in this album by virtue of the seven members that were released from shops in Brunswick green, three being Swindon-built, Nos.D1002/3/4, while Nos.D1035/6/7/8 were the first four to be built at Crewe. Perhaps it should be mentioned that due to the late-running building programme it was decreed that Crewe would construct Nos.D1030 to D1034 instead of Swindon and those four were among the last to enter traffic. These changes of policy were probably academic when the National Traction Plan was being drawn up in the late 1960s with a view to rationalising the fleet and the WR's hydraulic classes were identified as being non-standard and earmarked for early withdrawal. The first condemnations occurred in mid-1973 and the withdrawal programme would have proceeded much more speedily but for the chronic unreliability of the WR's stud of English Electric Type 4 Class 50s. The 'Westerns' were kept going largely by the ingenuity of staff at Laira depot who cannibalised withdrawn examples and even instituted a repainting programme to keep the fleet looking reasonably presentable but, even so, some locomotives ran in deplorable external condition with undercoat and priming paint visible on their bodysides. Seven members of the class just lasted into 1977 and the class finally bowed out on 26th February when Nos.D1013 *Western Ranger* and D1023 *Western Fusilier* double-headed a commemorative rail tour which was patronised by hundreds of admiring fans with many more at the lineside. *R.C. Riley*

Not surprisingly, few pictures of green-liveried 'Westerns' were submitted for inclusion in this album but here is a shot of No.D1037 *Western Empress* near Burnham on 17th September 1967. Out-shopped from Crewe works in August 1962, No.D1037 survived in service until May 1976 and it was eventually broken-up at Swindon in February 1977. *Western Empress* was one of only three 'Westerns' that were never painted in maroon, its livery being changed from green to 'rail blue' with small yellow warning panels during an intermediate repair at Swindon works. The locomotive was out-shopped from a further intermediate overhaul on 25th June 1971, emerging with full yellow ends, dual brakes and dual AWS equipment.
Rail Photoprints

English Electric Prototype 2,700hp Type 4 Co-Co

During 1962 three prototype main line diesel locomotives were on loan to BR for test purposes, Brush Traction's No.D0280 *Falcon*, No.D0260 *Lion*, which was a joint venture by various companies, and Co-Co No.DP2, an English Electric (EE Co.) product which entered traffic on the London Midland Region in May 1962. The diesel power unit used was the 16CSVT, an updated version of that employed on the EE Co. D200 series Type 4s, which was rated at 2,700hp at 850 rpm. The origins of the engine can be traced back to English Electric's 16 cylinder 16SVT engine that was originally introduced in LMS-designed Co-Cos Nos.10000 and 10001 which were built in the late-1940s.The six traction motors and bogies fitted to No.DP2 were completely interchangeable with those fitted to the same company's Type 3 and Type 5 locomotives already in service with BR. The machine weighed 105 tons, was 69 feet 6 in over buffers and was fitted with a train heating boiler and water scoop – BR was still in the steam age at that time. The mechanical design of No.DP2 closely followed that of the same manufacturer's 'Deltics' which enabled the axle load to be kept within the 18 ton limit specified by BR. No.DP2 covered 100,000 miles in revenue earning service without incident and in mid-July 1963 was transferred to the Eastern Region at EE Co's request to permit direct comparison with the 'Deltics'. During a six-week period it worked the 10.10am King's Cross to Edinburgh and 10.30pm back on Mondays to Saturdays with an additional short Sunday turn. The locomotive proved its reliability and ran up a record weekly mileage for BR diesels of 5,270 during which time it achieved the milestone of 200,000 miles of trial running. In this picture No.DP2 is seen approaching York at the head of a northbound train in the early 1960s. The locomotive was in a rather uninspiring all-over green livery at that time but its performance appears to have more than compensated for its somewhat drab appearance. *Rail Photoprints*

No.DP2 disguised as a 'Deltic'. The locomotive reportedly had the same bodyshell as a 'Deltic' apart from the large radiator ventilators on the sides. In 1965, after completing 360,000 miles in everyday service, No.DP2 was overhauled, repainted in 'Deltic' colours and diagrammed to work the 'Sheffield Pullman' to and from King's Cross. During this work electronic equipment was fitted, including a sophisticated wheel slip detection device. Sadly, on 31st July 1967 No.DP2 was involved in a very serious accident near Thirsk when hauling the midday King's Cross to Edinburgh train and regrettably there was considerable loss of life. Unbeknown to the driver, one of the wagons marshalled in the 02.40 Cliffe (Kent) to Uddingston (Glasgow) cement train, which was proceeding northwards on the adjacent slow line, had become derailed and No.DP2 ran into the obstruction at considerable speed. The locomotive was derailed and suffered severe damage to the leading nose and left hand side and was removed to York shed where it was sheeted over to deter onlookers. The consequences of the accident could have been really catastrophic had it not been for the quick reaction of No.DP2's driver who applied the emergency brake immediately he saw something was amiss with the freight working ahead on the adjacent track. No.DP2 was beyond economic repair, condemned in September 1967 and eventually dismantled by English Electric in October 1968. The power unit was reusable, however, and initially fitted to Type 4 Co-Co No.D417. In this portrait No.DP2 is seen at Leeds Central in February 1967 waiting to be coupled on the southbound 'Yorkshire Pullman'; the DMU on the right is a BRCW 'Calder Valley' unit. *David Mitchell*

Clayton 900hp Type 1 Bo-Bo

The Clayton Bo-Bo Type 1s, a class that BR certainly lived to regret. In 1960 BR had three classes of Type 1 diesel locomotive in traffic, the English Electric machines that first appeared in June 1957 and locomotives built by British Thomson-Houston and North British which were introduced in November 1957 and May 1958 respectively. In early 1961 the first mentioned class was already giving good service on the ER, LMR and ScR while the other two types were confined to the ER, mostly at sheds in the London area, where staff were struggling to overcome a multiplicity of recurring faults. All of these classes had long bonnets with the cab at one end and footplate crews were unhappy about the restricted vision available when working nose end leading, so BR decided to invest in a new design, hailed as the 'Standard Type 1', with a centrally placed cab offering improved visibility during shunting operations which was expected to overcome the crews' objections. An order for 88 900hp locomotives for use in the ScR was placed with the Clayton Equipment Co. while a further batch of 29 was ordered from Beyer Peacock for the ER and NER, thus giving a total of 117 machines. The first locomotive made its debut in September 1962 and deliveries continued until April 1965. The locomotives were powered by two 6ZHXL Davey Paxman 450hp six-cylinder horizontal engines, one being positioned on each end of the centre cab; each engine drove a separate generator which provided power to two traction motors. There were two exceptions however, Nos.D8586 and D8587, both of which had Rolls Royce engines. The locomotives weighed 68 tons, were 47 feet over buffer beams and had a maximum speed of 60 mph. It has to be said that the design team had incredible foresight because the locomotives could work in multiples of up to three units and this must have been their salvation on many occasions as the class's chronic failure rate soon became apparent. The class's appalling availability sunk to hitherto unknown depths and was as low as 60% on occasions and the first withdrawals took place in July 1968 just over three years after the final machine entered service. Amazingly, some locomotives survived less than five years in traffic and to make matters worse some footplate staff disliked the Claytons almost as much as the other Type 1s because their view was still partially obscured when shunting. In this photograph No.D8524 is seen at the almost deserted former shed at Tebay on 9th March 1968, the depot having closed from 31st December 1967 when Clayton diesels ousted steam locomotives on banking duties up to Shap summit. Steam traction north of Oxenholme was virtually a thing of the past by the date of this shot, the only steam turn being the 9.40am Horrocksford (Clitheroe) to Harrison's Sidings (Shap) and 1.50pm return which usually ran three days a week.
ARPT

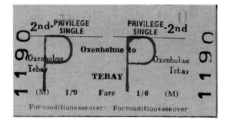

The Claytons were not originally intended for work on the LMR but 18 finished their careers (such as they were!) allocated to the Preston Division where they presumably operated side-by-side with the equally disastrous Metro-Vick Co-Bos. In this delightful scene, photographed at Cark & Cartmel on the fringes of the Lake District, Nos.D8509 and D8522 are seen hauling an eastbound special working on 21st June 1968. Note the leading locomotive is in green livery while the train engine is sporting corporate blue. Both locomotives were withdrawn in October 1968 and were eventually cut-up in Glasgow in 1972. *RCTS Archive*

Type 1 Bo-Bo No.D8590 wheels a southbound freight working through Newcastle Central on 17th June 1968. This locomotive was a Beyer Peacock product and entered service at Thornaby shed in May 1964 but had a working life of less than seven years being withdrawn from Gateshead in March 1971. The locomotive in the distance on the left is BR/Sulzer Type 2 No.D5148.
Terry Phillips

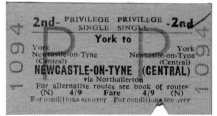

Brush 2,750hp Type 4 Co-Co

The Brush Type 4s - BR's maids of all work. In early 1961 BR placed their first order for 20 Type 4 Co-Co locomotives with Brush Traction, part of the Hawker-Siddeley group, and at first the locomotives were known as the Hawker-Siddeley Type 4s but later the description Brush Type 4s became widely accepted. These machines were the first production locomotives to be powered by Sulzer's pressure-charged, air-intercooled, diesel injection 12LDA-28C engine which had been uprated to 2,750hp. This engine was installed in No.D0260 *Lion*, an experimental locomotive that started main line trials in April 1962. BR was apparently very reluctant to release details of subsequent contracts, but in late 1962 information leaked out that a further 83 engines had definitely been ordered and 'informed sources' indicated that as many as 200 locomotives were scheduled to be built by Brush and Crewe works. A huge total of 512 machines was

eventually constructed between September 1962 and January 1968, divided between Brush, which built 310 at Loughborough, and BR at Crewe. The locomotives were the best of both worlds from BR's point of view because they were much lighter than the existing Type 4s in service and considerably more powerful – the 2,000hp English Electric Type 4s, for example, weighed 133 tons compared to the Brush Type 4's 114 tons with variations. The overall length of the locomotives was 63ft 6ins., they had six Brush traction motors, two 850 gallon fuel tanks and a top speed of 95mph. The British Transport Commission Design Panel advised on the external design of the locomotives, the livery being BR standard Brunswick green bodywork with a striking broad band of olive green. In this photograph No.D1853 is depicted at Bangor hauling the 11.45am Euston to Holyhead train in July 1965 when it was almost brand new, having been delivered from Crewe works during the previous month. *Chris Evans*

The 1960s saw the inauguration of BR's Freightliner network and in this portrait a southbound working is seen descending Beattock bank behind Brush Type 4 No.D1635 in June 1967. A Crewe-built machine, No.D1635 entered traffic in November 1964. *Rail Photoprints*

During the 1960s stations such as Oslo (Vippetangen) and Stavanger appeared regularly in the North Eastern Region public timetable in connection with sailings to Norway from Tyne Commission Quay near Newcastle-upon-Tyne. The ships were operated by the Fred Olsen and Bergen Lines and regular connecting services such as 'The Norseman' ran from London's King's Cross station some of which were solely for the use of international passengers. The journey from London to Oslo was clearly one for the most hardy and seasoned traveller because passengers leaving London at 9.20am on a Monday could not expect to arrive in Oslo until 7.15am on the following Wednesday. In this picture Brush Type 4 No.D1570 is seen departing from Tyne Commission Quay with the empty stock of the 9.00am from King's Cross on 24th February 1968. The photographer comments that the train had been hauled as far as Newcastle by sister locomotive No.D1991 where the portion destined for the quay had been coupled to other vehicles before setting off behind No.D1570. Remarkably, local tickets were issued and passengers wishing to travel between Newcastle and the quay did not require a boat ticket! This was the last full year of these locomotive-hauled workings which were replaced by DMUs in May 1969 apparently to allow the introduction of fixed formation Mk.2a sets on the East Coast route. A further downgrading occurred in May 1970 when the DMUs gave way to buses. *Terry Phillips*

The snowy wastes of Shankend. The Brush Type 4s were nothing if not versatile and in this portrait an unidentified member of the class is seen crossing Shankend viaduct, on the Waverley route, with a lightweight northbound freight train in December 1968. Sadly, this epic route was closed to passenger traffic amid a storm of protest from 6th January 1969 and large communities such as Galashiels and Hawick were left totally isolated, many miles from the nearest railway. When this 98¼ miles-long line was closed it was said to be the biggest loss maker in Scotland and the long section south of Hawick, which latterly only had six weekday trains per day, ran across empty, inhospitable moorland serving just a few villages with little traffic potential. The Waverley route was immortalised by the late Peter Handford who made night-time tape recordings of heavy, steam hauled freight trains blasting up the 1 in 75 gradient from Newcastleton to the lonely Whitrope summit. *Author*

More snowy wastes – this time at Durham. This shot, taken just north of Durham station on 8th February 1969, shows No.D1865 approaching with the 3.15pm Newcastle-upon-Tyne to King's Cross, running 20 minutes late, which is formed of a rake of mainly early Mk.2 vehicles. The photographer notes that this train was normally a 'Deltic' duty but heavy snow further south had disrupted traffic and presumably a Brush Type 4 was the most suitable power available. Note the coal yard on the left of the picture and large signal box that controlled movements at this end of the station. *Terry Phillips*

When deliveries of the Brush Type 4s commenced BR managers must have been delighted that they now had a very powerful, versatile locomotive with a wide route availability. No.1600, seen here passing Whitstable and Tankerton with the 7.45am Cardiff to Margate mystery excursion on 12th September 1971, demonstrates that versatility. The sun was shining as the train passed through Whitstable which augured well for a good day at the seaside. Perhaps the biggest mystery concerned the strange headcode (denoting a Class 4 train) being displayed by the locomotive – surely the train crew would have been given a Class 1 reporting number? *Terry Phillips*

When BR adopted its corporate blue livery in 1965 nobody expected that every item of rolling stock would be repainted overnight but eleven years later locomotives could still be seen in shabby green livery. In this picture Brush Type 4 No.47 256 is seen powering the 12.30pm Paddington to Paignton train near Aldermaston on 8th May 1976. This machine is thought to have been one of the last members of its class to retain green livery but locomotives of other classes were still sporting faded green long after the introduction of rail blue. *Chris Evans*

Swindon-built 650hp Type 1 0-6-0

The BR modernisation programme was beset with problems principally as a result of the haste with which it was implemented and multiplicity of untried locomotive designs that were sometimes ordered straight off the drawing board. While the railway enthusiasts of the day were doubtless fascinated by the diesels of various shapes and sizes, perhaps BR would have been wise to standardise on trusted General Motors products. One of the most catastrophic errors concerned the Type 1 locomotive classes, five types being in traffic by the mid-1960s of which only the English Electric (EE Co.) machines, which had been the first to be introduced in 1957, had been successful. The final Type 1 locomotive was the Western Region's (WR) hydraulic version, the first of which made its debut in July 1964, and this became yet another class to be added to the list of disastrous Type 1 designs. Twenty-six 650hp, 48½ ton locomotives (Nos.D9500 to D9525) with the 0-6-0 wheel arrangement were ordered from Swindon works in mid-1963 and, in keeping with WR tradition, hydraulic rather than electrical transmission was specified; a further order was placed for 30 locomotives. The power plant was a Paxman Ventura 6YJXL engine and the locomotives employed a Voith L217U transmission. The machines were built for yard and trip working and, unbelievably, they appeared just at the time this traditional form of railway working was contracting significantly. It was almost as if the traction planners were unaware of developments in the outside world! The majority of the locomotives theoretically lasted in BR service for about four years while No.D9531 appears to have had the briefest BR career, having being delivered in February 1965 and withdrawn in December 1967. What an accolade! BR cut their losses by selling the locomotives to heavy industrial users such as the National Coal Board and a fair number have subsequently found a further lease of life in preservation. Meanwhile the original Type 1 EE Co. design was still happily rolling off the production lines, the last example entering service in February 1968. The doyen of the hydraulic class, No.D9500, is depicted at Swindon works on 21st June 1964. *Rodney Lissenden*

A Morris Minor travelling on a Lowfit wagon, two wagons carrying containers and a busy goods depot in the background full of wagonload traffic. Sadly, the operation of railways was changing rapidly when this photograph was taken at Bedminster, Bristol, and the kind of traditional traffic for which the Type 1 0-6-0s were designed was not destined to last much longer. No.D9517 is depicted hauling a mixed goods working and this portrait was taken in August 1966. New in November 1964, No.D9517 was withdrawn in October 1968 and sold to the NCB for work at Ashington colliery in Northumberland. *Rail Photoprints*

Photographed on an appropriately gloomy day, No.D9524 poses at Cinderford, in the Forest of Dean, on 10th August 1967. The branch reportedly closed to goods working from 1st August and this was presumably the last working to remove remaining wagons. The line between Newnham (Bullo Pill West) and Cinderford lost its passenger trains from 3rd November 1958. No.D9524 entered traffic in December 1964, was made redundant by BR in April 1969 and subsequently sold for preservation. *Online Transport Archive*

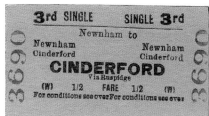

Diesel Shunters

The ubiquitous BR 350hp diesel shunter, introduced in 1952 and built in vast numbers until 1962, became one of BR's largest locomotive fleets and this has tended to overshadow the many smaller, less powerful classes sometimes built for specific tasks for which the larger machines were unsuitable. A large number of 204hp 0-6-0 shunters was produced and in this picture No.D2141 is seen at Culmstock hauling a Hemyock to Tiverton Junction milk train on 2nd September 1964; it is likely that the train's ultimate destination was somewhere in the London area. More than 200 of these diminutive locomotives were built by BR at Doncaster and Swindon while almost identical machines were also produced by Drewry. These locomotives incorporated a Gardner 8L3 engine, weighed 30 tons 16 cwt and had mechanical transmission. This particular example was built at Swindon and entered traffic in May 1960 at Taunton and finished its career at Landore, Swansea, in July 1985 so it had quite a long innings in contrast to other sister engines that were withdrawn in the late-1960s. The Tiverton Junction to Hemyock branch was famous in enthusiast circles as a result of its passenger service schedules where trains took 40 min. to cover the 7½ miles between those points. Passenger trains were withdrawn from 9th September 1963 and the line closed completely when the dairy at Hemyock closed in November 1975 and one of Great Britain's most attractive branch lines was lost. *David Mitchell*

Weymouth Quay was the departure point of ships sailing to the Channel Islands and in times past was very busy with connecting boat trains to and from Waterloo. The quay was some distance from Weymouth station, the two being linked by a tramway which was often worked at full capacity on summer Saturdays. Latterly, the tramway was worked by 204hp diesel shunters and in this shot an unidentified locomotive is seen on the quay on 6th September 1966. Locomotives that worked the tramway were fitted with a bell to warn pedestrians and this is just visible in front of the cab. Regular traffic is thought to have ceased in September 1987. *Terry Phillips*

The lure of famous diesel classes such as the 'Deltics' and 'Westerns' has meant that photographers were often drawn to scenic locations on the main lines and more mundane, everyday activities on the railway were neglected. In this photograph which is full of interest, two 0-4-0 shunters (No.D2950 is nearest to the camera) are seen at work in Ipswich docks on 16th May 1966. They were members of a small class of three locomotives built by the Hunslet Engine Co. in 1954/5 and were powered by a Gardner 6L3 153hp engine, weighed 22 tons 9 cwt and had mechanical transmission; they were originally numbered 11500/1/2 and later became Nos.D2950/1/2. The locomotives were based at Ipswich when new and appear to have spent almost all of their working lives in the docks. No.D2952 does seem to have been based at Ipswich for its entire career until withdrawn in December 1966, whereas the other two engines were transferred to Goole shed at about the same time – presumably their services were no longer needed at Ipswich. Nos.D2950/1 were eventually withdrawn from traffic in December 1967. Note that the locomotives are fitted with valances and cowcatchers as a safety precaution during roadside running. In the background men can be seen laboriously unloading wagons with cranes and transferring their contents to road vehicles, an aspect of the railway scene long since consigned to history. *Noel Machell*

'British Rail regret that owing to a train failure in the West Jesmond area services may be subject to delay or cancellation'. On 6th March 1967 a BR/Sulzer Type 2 failed at West Jesmond while hauling a breakdown train and 350hp diesel shunter, No.D3073, was commandeered as a replacement with a view to clearing the line as soon as practicable. The shunter had insufficient braking power for the steep falling gradient between West Jesmond and Manors so a following, empty 9-car DMU was attached to provide the necessary brake force and the cavalcade is depicted at Jesmond. There were further difficulties with the train at Newcastle which resulted in some dislocation to the evening peak service and consequent late running. The 6th of March (as luck would have it!) just happened to be the first day of mixed EMU and DMU operation on the North Tyneside lines preparatory to the elimination of electric traction so the staff in the local traffic control office must have been kept busy that evening. Jesmond station was closed from 23rd January 1978 to enable work to commence on the Metro and was replaced by a nearby underground station in August 1980. *Terry Phillips*

Opposite right: BR's 350hp diesel shunters penetrated virtually every part of the system excepting, perhaps, the most tightly curved or lightly laid sidings where only smaller locomotives were permitted. The design was based on that of the LMS shunters introduced in 1945 and construction of the BR version covered the ten-year period from 1952 and involved five different BR workshops but none was constructed by outside contractors. These 0-6-0 locomotives were fitted with six cylinder engines, either an English Electric (EE Co.) 6KT or Blackstone ER6T, and those engines powered respectively two EE Co. or GEC traction motors. There were slight variations in the weight of the machines between the earlier locomotives which weighed 49 tons, and the later ones which averaged 47½ tons. It should be noted that there were some small non-standard batches, such as the 10 machines fitted with Crossley engines and 15 equipped with British Thomson-Houston traction motors, but they were withdrawn in the late-1960s. The contraction of BR's wagonload freight business resulted in a dramatic fall in the number of goods depots which in turn reduced shunting requirements and consequently large numbers of 350hp shunters were made redundant and withdrawn. In this picture No.08 306 is seen acting as station pilot at Huddersfield on 2nd August 1974. This locomotive was a product of Derby works, being out-shopped in August 1957 and it survived in service until December 1977. *Chris Evans*

A long train for a little engine. An Andrew Barclay Co. diesel shunter, No.D2442, appears to be doing its best hauling a coal train through Dysart station, near Kirkcaldy, on 7th August 1969. BR had a bewildering variety of small diesel shunters from no fewer than nine manufacturers and this particular locomotive was one of a fleet of 35 introduced in 1958 for use on the Scottish Region. Equipped with a Gardner 8L3 engine, these 204hp machines were fitted with Vulcan-Sinclair mechanical transmission and weighed 35 tons; they had a maximum speed of 23mph. Some of these shunters survived no more than seven years in service but others lasted more than 20 years, perhaps employed on lightly laid, tightly curved tracks where they were indispensable. The last survivors were shedded at Dundee, presumably for use in the docks, and were taken out of traffic in early 1981. *Rail Photoprints*

Southern Region Diesel-Electric Multiple Units

The Southern Region's (SR) DEMU fleet encompassed no more than 75 units but this modest fleet had a fascinating and complex history and included units specially constructed with narrow bodies for use on routes with restricted clearances. The unit depicted here is No.1012 (classified 6L by the SR) a six-car formation built with flat sided bodywork for use on the Charing Cross/Cannon Street to Hastings route via Battle where narrow tunnels precluded the employment of standard width stock; this picture was taken on 13th June 1959 at Cannon Street. This particular unit was released in May 1957 from Eastleigh Carriage works and lasted almost 30 years in service. The original number series of this stock was 1011 to 1019 and almost all of these units remained in service until withdrawn in May 1986 when the Hastings line was turned over to full electric working. The 6L units were formed with one Driving Motor Brake Second Open coach at each end flanking three Trailer Second Open Lavatory carriages and a Trailer First Lavatory (with a side corridor) providing a total of 48 first and 240 second class seats. It should be noted that unit Nos.1001 to 1007 (classified 6S) were similar, but built on short 57 feet long underframes that were originally intended to be used for locomotive hauled stock; consequently they had a lower seating capacity. Each motor coach was equipped with a 500hp English Electric (EE Co.) 4SRKT engine mounted above the underframe in a purpose built engine room and this supplied power to two EE Co. 507 type traction motors. The motors were fitted to the bogie at the inner end of the vehicle in order to minimise the weight carried by the bogie at the outer end which was immediately beneath the engine. The SR had considerable experience of electric traction and a long association with English Electric, so it was no surprise when they opted for diesel electric units, using tried and tested equipment, rather than diesel mechanical units that were being introduced elsewhere on the BR system. The fleet was based at St. Leonards depot which was situated close to the sea shore and constant exposure to the sea air (and sea spray on stormy days!) resulted in extensive body corrosion and units spending protracted periods under repair at Eastleigh works. In addition, four vehicles from unit No.1007 were written off following the Hither Green disaster in November 1967 and these problems resulted in extensive reforms in order to keep the train service running – after all it was not possible to substitute any other rolling stock. Unit No.1001 has been preserved and makes frequent forays onto the national system on rail tours. *R.C. Riley*

During 1957 Eastleigh Carriage works constructed 18 2-car diesel electric units (Nos.1101 to 1118) for use on various services in Hampshire and they were classified 2H by the SR. The units were basically a diesel version of the 2-HAP electric units that were being built concurrently and each consisted of a Motor Second Brake (MSB) and a Driving Trailer Composite (DTC). Four more units (Nos.1119 to 1122) were built in mid-1958 for the Ashford to Hastings line and in the following year a batch of Trailer Seconds was produced to increase the seating capacity of the existing Hampshire units which were unable to cope with a dramatic surge in patronage. The fleet was further augmented by four more 3-car units (Nos.1123 to 1126) in 1959/60 while dieselisation of the Reading to Salisbury route and Fawley branch prompted the construction of seven units in 1962 (Nos.1127 to 1133) which were frequently referred to unofficially as the 'Berkshire' units. All of the units were powered by an English Electric 4SRKT engine which provided power to two 507 type traction motors. The MSB vehicles seated 52 passengers (with variations) while the capacity of the DTC coaches was generally 13 first and 50 second class seats but it should be noted that there were considerable differences between batches. In this picture unit No.1122 is seen climbing away from Alton with a Southampton service in 1967; the leading vehicle is the DTC coach. This unit was originally built for the Ashford to Hastings service, as previously stated, but was transferred to Eastleigh in May 1964 and, together with No.1121 which arrived at Eastleigh a little later, monopolised the Alton line trains until closure in 1973. The section of line between Alton and Alresford was taken over by a preservation society and is still very much in use today. *ARPT*

An interim diesel service was introduced on the Hastings line from 17th June 1957 using a mix of steam and diesel traction but the first DEMUs were rushed into traffic earlier than expected following a serious fire at Cannon Street signal box. The operating authorities were anxious to minimise movements in the station area, hence the use of the brand new units in which the management clearly had total confidence – there were no sophisticated electronic gimmicks in those days just simple and robust equipment that did the job. The full DEMU operated train service along the Hastings line commenced on 9th June 1958 and by that time further stock had been delivered in the shape of seven buffet units (classified 6B) and numbered 1031 to 1037. These units were identical to the 6L sets but had a buffet marshalled towards the centre of the unit in place of a Trailer Second; the buffet car had unclassified seating for 21 passengers. Passengers entered the vehicles through pairs of inswinging gangway doors there being no external doors for passengers' use. The units were often reformed to provide the maximum number of

coaches in traffic, but this objective was hampered by units spending a long time under repair at Swindon works in the late 1970s and a destructive derailment at Appledore in March 1980 which resulted in one of No.1033's motor coaches being written off. Buffet facilities were withdrawn from the Hastings line in May 1980 and the 6B units eventually reduced to five cars and re-classified 5L. In this picture unit No.1034 is seen at London Bridge on 14th May 1959, the third vehicle, which can just be discerned, being the Trailer First with doors to each compartment. *R.C. Riley*

Maintaining the Fleet

When this photograph of King's Cross fuelling point was taken on 28th September 1966 the age of the High Speed Train was still a very long way off and 'Deltics', Brush Type 4s and English Electric Type 4s held sway on the ECML expresses. While the primary purpose of this installation was to re-fuel locomotives, it is likely that the local King's Cross station fitter made frequent visits to diagnose faults and rectify minor defects where possible. Locomotives on display include 'Deltic' No.D9013 *The Black Watch*, two Brush Type 4s, two Brush Type 2s and a 'Baby Deltic'. Despite the eclipse of steam traction there was still much to interest the enthusiast in contrast to the dull uniformity of today's multiple unit trains. *Terry Phillips*

A general view inside Doncaster works on 16th June 1967 with a variety of locomotives undergoing overhaul. Those locomotives visible include (from l. to r.) Brush Type 2 No.D5817, 'Deltic' No.D9008 *The Green Howards* in the distance and a British Thomson-Houston Type 1 Bo-Bo. The latter machine was from one of BR's most unreliable diesel classes and no doubt a regular visitor to the works who were expected to remedy its 'incurable' problems. *Terry Phillips*

One of the most unfortunate aspects of the Modernisation Plan was the failure to build suitable maintenance facilities which sometimes resulted in steam and diesel locomotives being maintained side by side. When this shot was taken at Polmadie shed in May 1968 steam had only recently been banished from Scotland and the building depicted here is still soot-encrusted and hardly an ideal advertisement for BR's modern image. *Eastbank Model Railway Club*

The author well remembers visits to Crewe works in the early 1960s when a vast array of steam power could be seen being overhauled, but one of his clearest recollections was the sad sight of 'Patriot' Class 6P5F 4-6-0 No.45509 *The Derbyshire Yeomanry* in the early stages of being broken-up. When this shot of the interior of the works was taken on 10th May 1970 the age of steam had passed and the most interesting locomotive type that could be seen (at least in the author's opinion!) were English Electric Type 4s, the example seen here being No.D285 which had been in traffic almost ten years by this time. No.D285 later earned a footnote in the history books when, as No.40 085, it powered one of the final scheduled freight trains along the Settle and Carlisle line in May 1983. Two English Electric Type 3s are undergoing repair on the same road as No.D285 while a Brush Type 4 is visible on the left of the shot. *Rail Photoprints*

Tailpiece

A stranger in Sussex. A 'Derby Lightweight' single unit No.RDB975010, formerly Driving Motor Brake Second No.M79900, crosses the Ouse Valley viaduct, between Haywards Heath and Balcombe, on 28th July 1998. This single car was built at Derby in 1956 and began active life on the Bletchley (Verney Junction) to Banbury branch, one of two units specially constructed for use on that line in an attempt to reduce costs and increase patronage. Alas, the line was still deemed to be uneconomic and was closed despite a massive turnaround in its financial fortunes. Following withdrawal in October 1967 No.M79900 became a route-learning car on the ER and was subsequently acquired by the Railway Technical Centre, Derby, for conversion into a mobile laboratory who re-numbered it and bestowed the name *Iris*. The viaduct was undergoing refurbishment at the time, hence the high scaffolding on each side. The viaduct, which has 37 arches and is 1,475 feet-long, was completed in 1841 and no fewer than 11 million bricks were reputedly used in its construction. The contract price for the construction of this splendid Victorian masterpiece was £38,500.
John Goss L.B.I.P.P.

Back Cover: The prominent station nameboard leaves no room for doubt about the location of this picture which depicts Brush Type 2 No.5518 coming off the tightly-curved Harwich Parkeston Quay branch with the 6.33pm boat train to Liverpool Street on 17th June 1972. Corporate blue livery was making an impact across the system at this time; however, No.5518 still retained green livery but a double arrow symbol had replaced the BR 'lion and wheel' totem. One wonders if somebody had misread the corporate livery instruction manual!
Terry Phillips